While Swans Fly *and* Herons Wait

Sarah Dickinson

While Swans Fly *and* Herons Wait

Sarah Dickinson

Bramdean Press, 16 Granary & Bakery, Royal Clarence Yard,
Weevil Lane, Gosport, PO12 1FX, UK
ISBN 978-0-9557805-2-3

Cover painting by Michael Samson: www.michaelsamson.co.uk
Cover painting photographed by Ian Shewan: ianshewan.com
Photograph on page 28 by Ian Shewan
Photograph on page 73 by John Reid
All other photographs taken by and copyright © of Sarah Dickinson
Designer: Lizzy Laczynska – xhtdesign@googlemail.com

For

James, Sam, and Andrew

Contents

Preface

The book in your hands is an invitation to explore contemplative prayer and to discover its riches as a way to deepen your walk with God. It introduces and makes the case for contemplative prayer drawing on parts of my life story and, therefore, my personal experience of how it has helped me on my journey.

Throughout the book there are boxed sections which are opportunities for you to *pause and reflect.* My hope is that these sections will lead you by gradual and easy steps into the experience of contemplative prayer when you follow them as guided.

They are an invitation to have a go; perhaps even to let the rhythm of your reading be *interrupted* for a while. They echo the way that God might seek at times to interrupt any one of us by pointing our attention to something we would not notice unless nudged to have another look. Contemplative Prayer encourages a walk that is open to such invitations even when it means a slower pace.

However, you do not have to do the reflections. They are, of course, optional. I would encourage you though, at the very least, to read these boxed sections as they contribute to the story I am telling. You can always come back to consider their invitation at a later date. They are listed in Appendix 9 so that you can easily find them again.

Reading the reflections will also give you an insight into how I practise the discipline of contemplative prayer and in the process, I hope, reveal just how accessible this type of prayer actually is.

The bible quotes throughout the book are taken from the New International Version of the Bible unless otherwise indicated. Although I have other bible translations, this was the bible that I carried with me and used most during the years and experiences related.

This book centres on a period in my life when I felt God by his Spirit guiding and leading me to a deeper understanding and experience of who He was. It was a time when I was particularly aware, as I practised the discipline of contemplative prayer, of God's grace and presence with the growth that can bring. However, I would not want to mislead the reader into thinking that there are never dry times for me. Although I have never personally experienced the desolation of having no sense at all of God's presence – a spiritual reality attested to by many faithful believers over the centuries – I do know, of course, the arid periods that we can all experience on our faith journeys. My faith is not extraordinary; God's faithfulness, on the other hand, is.

Sarah Dickinson, November 2016

Chapter 1

Black Monday

'You are not to go back to sleep.' As I hear the instruction, my eyes take in legs in what appear to be green overalls. I open my eyes wider as she speaks to me again, 'You are not to go back to sleep. You *must* stay awake.' Beyond her green legs, I can make out my husband sitting and looking at me. Did he smile? Did he speak? I don't remember. My mind was too busy trying to make sense of where I was and what was happening.

It had been a Monday morning; the first Monday morning of the winter school holidays. We were setting off by car from our home in the north east of Scotland to see my family for Christmas in the south west of England. On Boxing Day, we were going to travel on by air to Switzerland for a week's skiing with friends. We: my husband, James, my two teenage sons, Sam and Andrew, and me.

It had been a fine morning despite forecasts that bad weather and snow were expected over the day ahead. Indeed, although cold, it had been clear and bright as we had loaded the car. We departed with the weather still on our side.

Sam, with his long legs, had been sitting in the front next to James who was driving. Andrew and I were in the back. We had been only a few miles from home on a straight stretch of dual carriageway next to open fields when the day had taken its dark turn. The sun was shining but there was black ice on the road. The

11

car had swayed and, in the moments it took to register the danger, we were already heading off the carriageway and down a small embankment. The car had punched through a fence and rolled once before landing back on its wheels. As it was happening I had thought 'this is not good', and I had been right.

I had and have no memory of the car actually rolling. My recollections of what happened in that field are extremely limited even now. They begin with the door next to me opening.

> I fell through it and down on to the ground. I put my right arm out to brace myself against the fall and noticed that I had hurt my arm in some way because my hand was red and purple with bruising. I looked into the car and saw Sam leaning to one side but clearly alert and alive. James, standing above me, was leaning on my open car door speaking to the emergency services. I heard him giving directions and remarking that someone was already approaching when Andrew helped me up, and we walked away. I looked back, registering as I did so, that the car had definitely rolled; the shallow dent in the roof said as much.

My memories to this day end there. I do not remember where Andrew actually took me, nor can I summon up images of the arrival of police cars, fire engines, and ambulances. I can recall nothing of that at all.

'You are not to go back to sleep.' The instruction comes for a third time, and this time I look at her and take in her green paramedic uniform. I realise I am on a stretcher in an ambulance and, although James is with me, the boys are obviously not. I listen to the vehicle as it heads the twenty or so miles back to our local hospital. I want to sleep.

Where were the boys? Why was James with me and not them? What had happened?

Snow is falling as we arrive at the hospital and, although I do not yet realise it, we are in fact together; one family, three ambulances.

There was no waiting around at Accident & Emergency. The doctors moved quickly to take stock of our injuries whilst James, unhurt, moved between the three adjacent cubicles where we were being seen. Mine were eventually established as minor; limited mostly to a dislocation of the right shoulder. Andrew, although admitted with bleeding around his ears and associated concerns that he had head injuries, was in fact fine. It was Sam who was seriously hurt. There was barely a mark on him and yet damage all through him touching him everywhere. The C5 vertebra in his neck had broken and dislocated as we rolled. My seventeen-year-old son was now tetraplegic. He had paralysis affecting the core of his body and all four limbs.

Sam was taken to the High Dependency Unit soon after our arrival at the hospital. Meanwhile, Andrew and I were settled in the Accident & Emergency ward to have our injuries investigated and treated further. It was only much later on that first day that I was put in a wheelchair and taken up to see Sam.

I clearly remember arriving next to his bed. His body was not visibly broken; there was neither plaster cast nor bandaging to signal injury just a massive weight which, attached to his head, was hanging down over the top end of the bed. It drew and kept the head back in the hope of taking some of the pressure from the broken vertebra off the swollen spinal cord. His body looked intact no matter that he could not move a limb. When he spoke to me, I knew immediately that his mind was intact. Most importantly, though, it was clear that his spirit was intact. His first words to me were, 'I am still leaving home.'

Only three days before the accident Sam had heard that he had a conditional offer to read Philosophy, Politics and Economics at Oxford. He had wanted to go to Oxford for as long as I could remember and he had worked consistently towards this goal while at school.

The application process to Oxford includes not only the usual university application forms but also the additional hurdles of an Oxford set and course specific exam, the results of which determine whether the applicant is then further called for interview. Sam had returned from his interviews on a massive high. Inevitable nerves aside, he had loved his few days there and so, once he knew he had a conditional place, he was flying with his feet off the ground. He just needed to nail his final school exams. A bad case of paralysis was apparently not going to be allowed to interfere with fulfilling this particular dream.

Sam's response to his injury spoke volumes. This was a setback in his life journey but it was not going to stop him. He would still move forward come what may. Of course, on that first day, it is possible that he did not fully appreciate all the implications of the injury. The effects of paralysis are so much greater than simply not walking.

The exact implications for each person with spinal cord injury will vary depending on exactly which nerves in their central nervous system have been damaged and at what level of the spinal column. Neck injuries will usually result in tetraplegia with all four limbs affected whereas a lower back break will affect the lower limbs of the body leading to paraplegia. However, in both instances, there will be loss of control over bladder and bowel function, sexual function and body temperature control will be impacted, and sensory awareness – whether light touch or the ability to discern and distinguish blunt/sharp impacts – will also usually be affected. Core strength being altered so too is stamina; you just won't have the energy you used to.

BEFORE YOU GO ON, imagine suddenly losing nearly all movement below the shoulders in the space of a few moments with all the associated dependency and life-altering changes that brings.

'I am still leaving home.' Was it the morphine coursing through his system that was doing the talking? It may have been. However, Sam has said since that he knew straight away in the car what had happened to him and, as he laid claim to his future that evening, he knew already the reality of a body that would no longer respond.

Sam's reaction amazed me. If he had lain there crushed in spirit or consumed with anger, or simply overwhelmed with grief, I would have completely understood. However, he neither appeared to then nor, as time would reveal, would he do later. Whatever Sam may have felt in the long watches of the night and as the days unfolded which, I am sure, included a wide range of normal emotions including fear and uncertainty, his first instinct had been to declare his belief and confidence in the life before him. I don't know what I would have expected of him. However, I don't think I would have anticipated such an immediately determined response, and not because prior to the accident there was anything to suggest otherwise. Rather because it begs the question of how we can ever really presume to foresee someone's actual response to such an event.

My own response caught me by surprise too. The day before the accident, if you had told me that 24 hours later my son might never walk again and had asked me how I would react, I would have said, 'Panic – if in doubt, panic.' You probably would not have believed me because I generally communicate confidence and strength. However, although the expectation would not have been completely without foundation, the inner reality of how I feel may be different at times to the image I am projecting. Fear especially is a foe that I know well regardless of any apparent self-confidence.

I have moved house over twenty times in my 53 years and have moved between countries twelve times.[†] I learnt – because I had to – from a young age to navigate the associated changes of culture and environment these moves brought with them; adapting to new schools or workplaces, making new friends, learning new languages, mixing in different social circles, and so on. These all presented not only opportunities for growth but also brought risks of rejection or failure. I can look back and see that I didn't really question my ability as a young girl to cope with these challenges. They were simply there, and I got on with them.

---

† Eight of those house moves and five of those country moves were in the first eighteen years.

However, I can also discern an unconscious choice as I got older about how to hold myself. I felt safest in myself when I was in control and so my modus operandi was to project confidence and hide, as far as possible, any fears or vulnerability I might actually feel when in a new or demanding situation. If you get enough practice at something it becomes a functioning reality. My confidence for coping with change did develop because change not stability was the norm. My confidence was not built, though, on a strong and stable foundation and I knew that.

Change for me, therefore, was both friend and enemy. On the one hand, it was exciting and brought new adventures and opportunities which I loved and, on the other hand, it meant a lack of real roots and the associated fear that, if you scratched my confident surface, I was actually extremely fragile and vulnerable. The thought of Sam being paralysed would have touched my very deepest fears of being overwhelmed. Inner if not outer panic would definitely have seemed to me one possible response.

As it happened though, I did not become hysterical or obviously panic which is not the same as claiming that I did not cry or was not devastated. I cried many hot tears and was profoundly distressed that Sam was afflicted in such a cruel and life-altering way. However, the accident gradually revealed a deeper truth than my fears had allowed me previously to perceive.

Although my life had involved constant uprooting as I moved from place to place, I had all the while been laying down roots in the geography of one singular place – faith in a loving and good God had been drilling its way down in my heart. I just didn't realise how strong or deep those foundations actually were because nothing had previously subjected me or my Christian faith to such intense challenge. I discovered that I could say with the psalmist the opening verses of Psalm 62:

Truly my soul finds rest in God;
  my salvation comes from him.
Truly he is my rock and my salvation;
  he is my fortress, I will never be shaken.

FOUNDATIONS

Jesus is very clear that we need good foundations because in life there will be storms and floods which will shake us. It is not a matter of if but when they will come. Therefore, Jesus tells us how to lay foundations which will enable us to withstand their onslaught.

Luke 6:46 – 48

Why do you call me, 'Lord, Lord,' and do not do what I say? As for everyone who comes to me and hears my words and puts them into practice, I will show you what they are like. They are like a man building a house, who dug down deep and laid the foundation on rock. When a flood came, the torrent struck that house but could not shake it, because it was well built.

I would invite you to take a few minutes to visualise the following:

📖 someone actually digging foundations for a house into rock

📖 the completed house

📖 the storm and rising flood waters

☩

Now with thought to this house you have visualised resisting the torrent, I would invite you to read the passage again

☩

Share in prayer with Jesus the response that comes forth in you, whatever that may be, to this passage.

☩

If you would like to reflect more deeply on your foundations, the reflection in Appendix 1 will enable you to do so using the imagery of the roots of a tree.

On that Monday morning, more than my arm was hurt; my heart was broken as well. Seeing my son injured in such a devastating way did make every fibre of my being howl in response. In those first days, still in hospital myself, I would lie there looking out the window as the snow continued to fall with my thoughts flitting about all over the place. My mind would circle round the details of the accident that I could remember, the unfolding implications for Sam, and the stream of associated questions which inevitably rose to the surface to probe my faith before looping back to a basic measure of relief and gratitude that we were all alive.

One minute I would be thinking inevitably about the 'what ifs': what if the snow had started falling heavily before we had left that morning, would we have left anyway when we did or would we have delayed our departure? What if my husband, driving below the speed limit, had been driving even slower? What if I had been sitting in the front seat and Sam in the back? What if we had left a few days earlier? What if, as 'good Christians', we had prayed specifically before we had set out for safety on the road? Would that have made a difference? Does God work like that?

The next minute my mind would be on to the 'whys'. Why should this happen to us? Why, when it was already well past the rush hour and so many cars would already have been over this busy road on a working Monday morning, would our car have been affected by this ice? Why had Sam been hurt and not me? Why could it not have been me? If, by His Holy Spirit, God is with us always, where was He when my son's neck was broken? If He was there, why had this happened? Had He allowed it? What is the nature of His sovereignty in this world and does it actually require me to believe that, whether actively or passively, He determined or accepted that we should be rolled over in a field?

Such questions could only lead on to wondering whether this was some kind of punishment and then trying to work out which bit of sin in my life or my son's life, or my husband's life could possibly merit such affliction. What could possibly have been done or said to deserve this kind of outcome? Old Testament stories of God chastising Israel for its sin sit in tension with the New Testament account of the reply Jesus gives to a question about a man who has been blind from birth.

John 9:2–3

His disciples asked him, "Rabbi, who sinned, this man or his parents, that he was born blind?"

"Neither this man nor his parents sinned," said Jesus, "but this happened so that the works of God might be displayed in him."

How these tensions are held together and worked out is difficult enough with a clear head; it is almost impossible with a befuddled one. I could not keep scary and confusing thoughts such as these completely out, but ultimately I did not believe that the loving God I felt I knew could be punishing Sam in this manner either.

My 'why' questions did also lead on to, 'and why not'? The laws of physics that keep us all with our feet on the ground are also those that caused the black ice to take our car off the road. Sam was not singled out to suffer; he was sitting in the most vulnerable seat in the car with nothing to protect him as we rolled rightwards towards the driver. His seatbelt held his body so his head and neck took the force of the roll. The movement of James' head was limited by the window next to him, as was mine, and between Andrew and I there was some hand luggage that possibly impeded his sideways movement. Sam had only the well between him and his father. There was nothing there as the car rolled over sideways to limit the movement of his head and neck. Whiplash broke Sam's neck. It was perfectly fathomable however awful its consequences.

Our accident did not need some kind of divine agenda to make sense. We live in a physical world governed by certain physical laws and dynamics. Things will happen. It would be a disorienting world if the laws of nature were not predictable and reliable.[†]

Also, I reasoned, why shouldn't something awful happen to us? Awful things are happening all the time. As I write, civil war is tearing Syria apart, Aids is still making orphans of children, and changing weather patterns are causing rising flood waters in one place and drought in another with devastating consequences for those affected. Hunger, poverty, joblessness, oppression, and mental and physical illness afflict and blight the lives of too many whether here in the United Kingdom or on distant continents. Suffering is part of the human experience and faith has to contend with it all the time.

I have never found the issue of suffering an easy one but nor has it been a faith limiting one. Prior to the accident, there were moments in my life when I would have wished things otherwise; when I hurt or someone I loved hurt. However, in the main I had had a comfortable, healthy, affluent, and fairly easy life. Suffering had not come stalking me in earnest even if I could see suffering was always on the rampage somewhere. Therefore, knowing suffering was on the loose and still finding it possible to love and worship God, surely, I felt, as I lay in my hospital bed, when it finally rocked up with steel-tipped boots and kicked down the doors protecting my little world, I should

---

[†] Even the black ice could be explained, I learnt later. That particular stretch of dual carriageway was open and exposed with little protection from wind. Black ice could form very quickly and last only short lengths of time. Passing low cloud most likely caused moisture to develop and blasts of cold air coming unimpeded across the fields froze it.

Our car very probably also contributed to what happened. Front wheel drive but heavily loaded at the back with luggage, we would have had less traction at the front and the car would have been less stable as we encountered the ice.

stand firm on that same faith.

'What if', 'why' and 'why not' were finally interspersed with thankfulness. I was immediately very aware of how fortunate we were to live in the United Kingdom. It was a genuine relief to know that whatever was happening and would still unfold for Sam, we did not have to add the anxiety of how we would pay for his treatment to the woes we were experiencing. I was also grateful that we had been so close to home rather than hundreds of miles away. Sam was so quickly transported to our local hospital and, although we had never had need of the hospital on this scale, we did know where we were. James was able to go home to his own bed and there was immediately a huge and practical outpouring of love and support from our church and community to sustain and encourage us.

We were also blessed that, within moments of our accident, a paramedic on his way back from another accident scene had indeed seen us and stopped. He had stabilised Sam's neck in a collar whilst making sure that he was not touched or moved inappropriately to limit the damage.

I was even grateful for my own injury. Without it I am quite sure that every maternal instinct would have led me to touch Sam in a way that would have caused him more harm. Having been led away from the car by Andrew, that risk had been avoided. There was much to be thankful for amidst the debris of all that had happened. These were reminders and signs of God's faithfulness and goodness; pointers to a God whose action in our lives is always saving and redemptive in nature.

There was much going on in my head over those early days as all these thoughts and questions came and went, and as I tackled a steep learning curve of information about spinal injury. My head was, in effect, in overdrive and I was too tired, too hurt, and too stunned by what had happened to be able to silence it or find peace from it. Thankfully though we are not just our mind and, therefore, not solely dependent on its wisdom and insight. Indeed, sometimes we can perceive things more clearly with our hearts, however shattered they may be.

Four days after the accident, when Sam was in intensive care following an operation to stabilise his neck, four friends came to see us one evening in hospital and suggested we go to its chapel to pray. James and I sat in a circle with these friends. I remember their presence not their words. I remember comfort. I remember hearing, beyond any spoken words, God's very quiet but clear invitation to trust Him. More specifically than that, I felt God lead me to a choice.

My heart was broken wide open and in anguish for Sam, which for me meant living with the ache of that pain as we journeyed forward with the consequences for him of his spinal injury. In response, I could close my heart tight against that pain, shutting it down and, thereby, keeping God out. Alternatively, I could carry the pain with His help and remain open to His love, which I would eventually see redeem and transform this tragedy.

I was simply unwilling to believe God had abandoned us. I was also unwilling to believe He had done this to us. However much my mind drew me to the inevitable 'what ifs' and 'whys', deep in my broken heart I never felt that God was part of the problem. I believed and wanted to believe God was at the heart of the solution. I believed God was good and that belief fundamentally informed time and again how I answered my own questions about God's role in what had and would happen.

This belief, indeed this active hope, did not just pop up out of nowhere. Over the previous twelve years, I had been exploring God's goodness completely unaware that I was preparing, in ways I could not have anticipated, for the events of that Monday morning. I knew the journey I had been on but I had no idea how much difference it would make when it mattered.

In that hospital chapel God spoke to my heart. He whispered an invitation to me to trust His capacity to transform what had happened.

Look at Sam's reaction. Is that not a marker of hope?

He was asking me to endure what I thought unendurable and to accept a vulnerability and real dependency on Him that did not come naturally to me.

The injury was asking the same things of Sam in even greater measure: endurance, vulnerability, and dependency.

Stay awake. Do not to go back to sleep.

God was asking me to remain attentive. If I did, I would notice His hand working for good in this; His love coming to me in tangible and practical ways.

If I would let Him work, the broken soil of my heart would be the place where new life would be seeded and grow. I only had to receive the life and hope that was offered.

Sam's broken body can be the place where new life can be seeded and grow too.

An invitation.

How to answer?

My heart heard the invitation. My head interpreted it. My soul whispered the barely audible response – 'Yes'.

Chapter 2

God is Good

S tay awake.

God declared Himself to be Yahweh when Moses allowed himself to be diverted by a burning bush as he tended his father-in-law's flock on Mount Horeb. He could have ignored it and moved on, but he didn't. He was attentive to it and, noticing that it did not burn up as it should, he went to investigate this strange sight further. His curiosity was rewarded with a divine encounter as God introduced Himself to Moses: "I AM WHO I AM"[†]

'I AM'. Not 'I Was' nor 'I Will Be' but 'I AM'. Although we may be able to point clearly to His presence with us in the past and be confident that His presence will remain with us into the future, the reality of God is now. However, we so often choose to live elsewhere than in the moment that is given. We dwell on the past wishing to relive its joys and high points or weighed down and held captive by its sorrows and regrets. Alternatively, we live for the future and what we are hoping for tomorrow that will be better or different. It is so hard to remain where we are and to live the fullness of that moment and yet that is where

---

[†]See verse 14 of Exodus 3:1–15.

we will find and encounter God; the One who says,

Jeremiah: 29:13

You will seek me and find me when you seek me with all your heart.[†]

In the wake of the accident, I believe God's call to me to stay awake and be attentive was so I might see Him at work to transform its aftermath. The more I was aware of Him alongside me, the more I would be comforted and strengthened to persevere in trusting Him however long that transformation took. I would need to bear with what the present held, painful though it was, because it was precisely there that God would reveal Himself. He would do so not only in that which was remarkable and hard to miss but in the mundane and ordinary too.

We may not all be dealing with the traumatic effects of spinal injury but we are all on journeys of transformation. As a result, I believe God invites us all to become more aware of His presence daily in our lives.

An example may help to explore this point further. What do I see when I take a bit of time to give the spoon below my full attention?

[†]See also Deuteronomy 4:29 when, in a similar vein, Moses says to the Israelites that it is when they seek God with all their heart and soul that they will find Him.

I see a machine-made object that has been shaped for a purpose which makes me wonder –

Am I, in effect, a machine-made cut-out or am I individually crafted?

What purpose might I have been fashioned for?

The spoon is made of stainless steel which is a strong material but one which can nonetheless, under enough pressure or stress, bend or even break.

What am I made of?

Would too much pressure or stress damage or break me?

The spoon has a handle which enables me to grip it comfortably without getting my hands dirty with the business end of the spoon.

What do I have a handle on?

What has a handle on me?

The spoon has a bowled end to it so that I can pick up a fluid or a solid.

What am I holding, if anything?

The spoon can be filled and it can be emptied.

How much am I holding?

If I am full, am I overflowing?

If I am empty, am I being replenished?

Is there a cycle or rhythm to how I am filled and poured out?

I can also use the spoon to stir.

What do I stir up?

What stirs me?

The spoon, if used, will get dirty and need cleaning to prevent harmful bacteria developing and building up on it with potentially noxious effects.

What is building-up on or in me, if anything?

Do I need cleansing?

Do I need purifying?

The humble spoon has much to say when we are fully awake to it and, as it reveals its insights, we can be changed by it. To be changed by a spoon may be surprising but then Moses was changed by a bush; a bush which revealed God Himself.

You may be thinking that it is not possible, moment by moment, to look at absolutely everything in life in such fine detail. You are right, of course. Nevertheless, we can live each moment much more expectantly and attentively than we often do for, as Paul reminds us there is:

Ephesians 4:6

. . . one God and Father of all, who is over all and through all and in all.

In other words, God is throughout His Creation at all times, present in all things. Furthermore, Jesus has promised to be with us always:

Matthew 28:20b

And surely I am with you always, to the very end of the age.

If we trust this to be true, we can be confident He is present by His Spirit in every moment of our day and will be active in our day if we let Him.

God will be the one to highlight something in the passing moment which requires closer attention; prompting us to slow down and have another, more careful, look. We just need to be willing to do precisely that. If we do heed the Spirit's nudge, we may discover that not only the extraordinary but also the ordinary moments and things we so often overlook and disregard are actually surprisingly full of revelation – or in other words, God.

SLOWING DOWN

Let's slow down now. The invitation is to take a few moments to focus on your breathing. Breathe normally to begin with. You might like to place your hand on your chest to feel its gentle lift and fall.

Then begin to breathe more deeply in and out. Feel your lungs fill with air as you exaggerate the movement of inhalation and feel them empty as you press all the air out.

What you can notice as you slowly do this are the moments of transition; the moments when our inhalation changes to exhalation and vice versa. These transitions reveal what are usually imperceptible gaps at the top and at the bottom of our breathing.

......➔

I like to imagine God is present in these gaps; with me, therefore, at the high and the low point of every breath. The gaps, although always there, are not noticeable when I am breathing normally; they become noticeable when I slow my breathing down.

✠

So it is also with God. Always present whether I notice or not but *more* noticeable when I move or breathe even just a little slower and make the space for Him just that bit bigger.

Slowing down, even a bit, to leave enough space to be attentive for God through our days is not easy, given the busy lifestyles most of us live. You might feel this would not come naturally to you; it certainly did not come naturally to me. However, it is a skill and subtle change of pace that can be learnt, as I want to demonstrate by sharing some of my own story with you.

There was a time when it was very unlikely that, in the day-to-day hurly-burly of my life, I would have been able to hear a gentle prompting from God's Spirit to be diverted so that He could reveal Himself to me. It was a time when I was so busy that the still quiet voice of God was daily in competition with the noisy racket my life was making; albeit much of this clamour came from church activities and well-intentioned pursuits. I also know that I was not really living in the expectation that God might be revealed at any moment in my day – yes, as an intellectual premise – but not in the reality of how I lived; there was no available gap for it.

However, this period of my life was to become pivotal in my faith journey. A walk which had started over twenty years before in a very slow way but, gaining steadily in momentum, had by then reached an unsustainable pace. I was well on target to smack into a wall of spiritual and physical exhaustion when God, reaching down in mercy, rescued me again.

The first time God saved me was in 1973 as an eleven-year-old in Canada. I came to faith through a bible study run by a friend's mother and fuelled by excellent homemade cookies. I learnt there what I think of as the essentials; that I was a sinner, that Christ loves me and died for me, and that by putting my faith in Him I would be saved.

Although christened as a baby in the Church of England, I did not come from a home with a church-going tradition and, although not in any way discouraged, neither was my faith actively developed at home. I had to find my own way. I read my bible, attended this weekly bible study, and very occasionally went to church with my friend. It was just enough to establish my faith and give it some basic roots.

When we moved to Argentina in 1976, my faith had only my personal bible reading to nourish it and this was periodic at best. It survived not because it was well tended but because it was not actively attacked. Also, God is faithful to us, if not always the other way round.

My final year of secondary education three years later was in France at a Catholic school run by nuns.† Regular biblical teaching and weekly attendance at mass gave some much needed and very

---

† The sisters were members of the Communauté Apostolique Saint-François-Xavier.

welcome nourishment to my faith which was then enriched further by a school trip to Israel and the Sinai. This three week pilgrimage brought the biblical narrative to life for me in ways that I still draw on today.

University in the UK followed and, although this might have been a time of growth, I must confess that I was more motivated by politics and, as a result, invested my time, energy, and passion in that.

It was not until I married James, also a Christian, at the age of 23 and we moved to Boston in the United States for 18 months, that my faith began to get consistent attention and nurture. By a route that has God's fingerprints all over it, we found ourselves, to our surprise, regularly attending a Brethren Assembly where we were challenged to take Scripture seriously even when it was uncomfortable. They had a far more literal interpretation of God's Word than we did or do now, but that did not matter. Those differences helped us to think more deeply about what we did believe and the implications of those beliefs for how we lived our daily lives.

As together we attended church and bible study regularly so we began to get involved with the church as the body of Christ – a people who love, comfort, encourage, and serve each other. This is an attractive vision and a powerful reality to experience.

It was inevitable, therefore, when we returned to England that we wished to remain involved. We joined a very lively Anglican evangelical and charismatic church in west London where we were then challenged to take seriously the power and action of God's Holy Spirit in our lives. I began to meet regularly with a friend to pray and James and I, by now, considered attending a bible study to be as normal and essential as attending church itself.[†] We did a leadership course whilst there too. We started up, soon after, a monthly lunch and games club for some of the local elderly residents.

Within a couple of years, we were offered a short nine month stint in Australia with James' work and, once there, found ourselves drawn to a Baptist congregation in Melbourne which had a strong emphasis on social justice and God's love expressed in action. Worship was not to be limited to the boundaries of Sunday services but was to find expression in how we offered up our lives daily in service to God. This simple but profound message has remained with me and challenged me ever since.

From Australia we moved to Belgium for three years where we worshipped again within the Anglican tradition at the Pro-cathedral in Brussels. This was a busy period for James and I in work terms as well as one of increasing activity in the church. We hosted and led a weekly bible study. We exercised the ministry of hospitality, and took seriously the call to use our gifts and talents. It was here that I learnt to appreciate the value of liturgy in worship, which united me with the many believers who through the ages had polished each word until it shone with meaning.

We returned to London from Belgium in 1993 to another Anglican church and carried on much as before except that we now had to factor in the impact and needs of small children as well. Therefore, a few years later in 1995, when we moved to Scotland with Sam,

---

[†]All our bible studies over the years have been what today would more likely be called a Home Group; a small group of Christians meeting to study God's Word, to pray and to encourage each other in their faith.

aged three, and Andrew, just fifteen months, we were pleased to find that our local Church of Scotland congregation had a lively ministry for children as well as being active in all the many other ways we had come to expect of a dynamic church.

The pattern of frequent moving had taught us to get involved quickly and to make the most of wherever we were at the time. As a result, we got stuck in straight away to doing what we could to be contributing members of Christ's body in the place we found ourselves. There were lots of ways to serve and lots of groups offering opportunities for fellowship and discipleship and within a couple of years, without really noticing, I was very busy. The problem was that this activity was leading to an imbalance between the pace and impact of what I will call horizontal versus vertical growth.

A faith that follows Jesus will always lead horizontally outwards towards others because His life did precisely that. However, Jesus was deeply rooted in His Father's will and models for us the equal necessity of time spent with the Father going deeper, vertically, in our relationship and dependence on Him.[†]

One Christmas, the way I decorated the mantelpiece in our living room reminded me of the balance required between the outer reach of our lives and this inner resourcing. In the middle of the mantelpiece I had placed a vase filled with ivy. I had cut very long strands so that the ivy could stretch from the vase to the end of the mantelpiece on either side. I chose the vase to ensure that the ivy could be deeply set in it to counterbalance the weight

---

[†]See Matthew 4:1–11; Matthew 14:13; Mark 1:35; Mark 14:32–36, Luke 5:16 amongst other passages.

of the ivy stretching along the mantelpiece.

To be full of life at the very far end of the mantelpiece, the ivy needed to be deeply and well held in the water at the centre. So it is with faith. We cannot extend our service and activity effectively without making time to go deeper in our faith as well or we risk falling out of the life-giving waters as the weight of what we do tugs us up, out, and down.

Although at the start of 1997 I would not have stopped to consider what a spoon might have to say to me, the spoon we were considering earlier, with the questions I suggested it might provoke, is actually very helpful in better understanding where I was spiritually at this point.

Had I reflected on a spoon in that way, it would have revealed that I believed I was individually crafted with a God-given purpose for my life for which the energy and endurance needed would be provided. Therefore, I might also have realised that I was not clear about what God's specific purposes for me actually were as all the activity in my life was only leading to unsustainable pressure and strain. Life, I might have noticed, had a handle on me, not the other way round. Also, I was increasingly depleted and empty with little time for the replenishment which might have enabled me to be poured out again.

When I look back on my life at that time, I can identify four strands to it. Overarching all was family life and, in particular, my time alongside James with the boys. We made it a priority to eat the meals we could together, to find time to play games together, to get out walking together, and so on.

I also had a lot of time with the boys on my own whilst James was at work, as I had chosen not to be in paid employment at this point. A good chunk of my day through the week, therefore, was taken up with their rhythms of play, learning, and rest. They were lively and active children but I still had time left to commit to other things alongside or around them.

The other two strands for the focus of my energies were church and politics.

It was an election year with all the campaign meetings, fundraising, and leafleting that entails and I was doing what I could locally to support those efforts prior to the General Election that May.

However, my church-related activities kept me the busiest. The list below gives you an idea of what I was up to weekly:

📖 co-leading one of three morning toddler groups (and chairing the committee that oversaw all three)

📖 helping with one of the Sunday School groups

📖 participating in a daytime discipleship course

📖 attending a mid-week ladies' fellowship group

📖 hosting an evening Alpha Course in my home for 24 people

Then to those weekly commitments the ones below can be added:

📖 hosting every other week an evening bible study

📖 helping out according to a rota in the church charity shop

📖 attending meetings of our church board which met roughly every six weeks to deal with property and finance issues, as well as

📖 attending meetings of its fundraising sub-committee

which resulted in helping with a wide range of different fundraising activities

📖 helping to photocopy the church magazine

📖 serving on one of the church welcome teams

📖 meeting to pray with two friends

WHAT ARE *YOU* DOING?

This was my list of church activities. It may prompt you to take a moment to reflect on what you are currently doing. If so, the invitation would be to invite God to guide your reflections as you do so. The aim here is not judgement but observation. However, if any thoughts would prompt you to action, I would encourage you to make a note of these but not to rush and act on them rather to hold them and wait further on God to confirm and lead you to any changes.

Obviously, I did not start out with twelve commitments. One by one they came up and, each time I was asked if I would like to be involved or if I could help, I said, 'yes'. Was I fashioned for all these different activities? Well, I could do them and, I hope, ably enough but I was probably a kitchen spoon also busy being a teaspoon, a dessert spoon, and a ladle.

Not all of these activities involved me in service; some were intended to encourage my personal and vertical growth as a Christian which they did. I began to keep a spiritual journal during this period as a result of the weekly discipleship course

I was doing. I used my journal to record insights, prayers, scriptures that challenged or encouraged me, hopes, questions, struggles, and disappointments. A repeated refrain in my journal from this period was that I was tired and low spiritually. Therefore, the investment that I was making in my relationship with Christ was producing some dividends; it was highlighting, if nothing else, that things were not right, that there was just too much activity going on to get it right.

Should I have been doing all these things? The answer is, of course, 'no'. Although I knew it would be wise to take the time to reflect and pray over how I directed my energies, I didn't – it is as simple as that. I was so caught up running at a certain pace and pitch, it seemed easier to do the next thing than it did to stop and seriously question what I was doing. I was clearly increasingly aware of the need to stop or slow down, I just didn't know how.

Also, if I am honest, I liked being busy. I liked in a prideful way that I seemed to be able to keep everything going whilst managing the demands of the boys and our family life. It made me feel good even as it tired me out. Life is often full of this type of paradox. I was also wary of letting people down or having them think less of me if I did less.

Thankfully, God is not only incredibly patient with our foolish ways but also compassionate and merciful.[†] In February 1997, I may not have been doing much prayerful listening to God but His Holy Spirit was nonetheless stirring within me and

---

[†]Nehemiah 9 offers a brief history of the Israelites which is worth a read for the rapid reminder it provides of just how compassionate and patient God is with our rebellious or foolish ways.

using the fatigue to get my attention. He did this, in particular, through a weekend retreat, which along the way introduced and explored the use of contemplation in prayer.[†]

At the start of the weekend we were encouraged to think about our hopes and desires for the weekend. This is what I wrote in my journal:

I am here –
📖 for a rest
  • to resource and nourish myself
📖 to recover some concentration
  • I am too tired
📖 to meet with God in prayer
  • to sort out a few priorities
  • to explore contemplative prayer

God's gradual response to these aspirations began with three words that the retreat leader repeated again and again over the weekend, **'God is good'**. These three words sounded out to me as though spoken in bold type every time she said them. **Pay attention to me**, they clamoured. I don't know if others that weekend were as acutely aware of them as I was but, with each repetition, they challenged me. I found myself not so much wondering if I believed them to be true, for I would have asserted them as true, but whether I lived as though they were true.

This thought, once planted, would not let me go. I reflected on

---

[†]The imagery of the spoon comes to mind again.

my life and felt that, although I might be able to talk about God's love and goodness, I just didn't live my life out of these truths.

It seemed to me that if you looked at all the busyness and spotted my associated tiredness, you might conclude that my God was a pretty hard taskmaster and not a particularly good one. Of course, one could point to any number of scriptures that would underline that this should not be true, including:

Matthew 11:28–30

Come to me, all you who are weary and burdened, and I will give you rest. Take my yoke upon you and learn from me, for I am gentle and humble in heart, and you will find rest for your souls. For my yoke is easy and my burden is light.

Given that Christ's obedience to the call in His life took Him to the cross, it does not follow from this scripture that the call of God is without challenge. However, as we follow where He would lead us, there is this assurance that we will be given the strength and the rest we need, that we will not fall or break under the weight of what is asked. God is good.

I was waking up to the fact that twenty-four years into my Christian journey with, by then, hours of sermons, bible studies, discipleship courses, spiritual reading, and conversations behind me, I had picked up a lot of knowledge about God. Some of this knowledge was vital, much of it was helpful, some of it was frankly baffling and mysterious. However, too much of it was ultimately sitting fairly comfortably in my head rather than in the depths of my heart from where it might bring about deeper change in me.

A helpful image here is that of a pillar candle. When the wick is first lit, the flame dances on the surface of the candle and brings a bright ambient light. Most of the rest of the candle meanwhile remains opaque and unaffected by that surface light.

However, over time, the flame burns down through the wax and, gradually, the dark base of the candle is transformed. The deeper that flame travels, the more the whole candle will be transfused with and transformed by the light of that flame.

Now consider the flame to be the knowledge of God as revealed in Christ. When we first receive that revelation, the flame is lit and that knowledge transforms us and brings light to our lives and that of others. This knowledge is always good but with time, ideally, it travels deeper in us. It takes root in our hearts as well; there where so much of the motivation for our actions comes from. When the heart is touched, the whole life has the potential to be lit up and transformed just like the whole candle is transformed.

HEAD AND HEART KNOWLEDGE

I would invite you to turn back to the images of the candles and to take some time to sit quietly with them. As you look at the images, ponder more deeply what they reveal and this potential for a gap between head and heart knowledge. Do so, not only in general terms, but also giving thought to how, if at all, that revelation speaks personally to you.

✠

I had a lot of knowledge by 1997 and yet my life was still waiting to be further transformed by the inner knowing that dwells in the heart. God had indeed saved me when I was eleven but now He was, in a sense, going to do it again. He was going to reveal His goodness to me afresh by teaching me the timbre of His voice so that I might hear Him when He called me to follow; a call which always leads to abundant life.[†]

The retreat weekend challenged me to question the motivating force behind all the activity in my life because I was clearly not solely responding to the Good Shepherd's voice. The Good Shepherd would not lead me to a place of absolute exhaustion but along a route that included still waters and green pastures.[*]

I did not experience these insights as judgement but as mercy and as an invitation to change. However, I couldn't work it out on

---

[†]See John 10: 1–10 but, in particular, verses 3, 4 & 10.
[*]See John 10:11 & Psalm 23.

my own. I did not have the built-in wisdom for that. I knew I would need God to keep leading me through this process. Fortunately, God is good, and the weekend didn't just provoke questions and throw down challenges, it offered me a way to begin exploring for some answers too.

Also, although I didn't realise it at the time, it was God's first invitation to me to stay awake. It is ironic then that the tool that would help me so much was one which sometimes involved shutting my eyes: contemplative prayer.

Chapter 3

Stop, Look, and Listen

Imagine for a moment that you were out shopping for spiritual disciplines and you came to a shelf of tins marked with the label contemplative prayer. What would you expect to find in the small print on the tin? Would it be something like this?

> **Exclusive offer!** This is prayer for the rare few who can subdue the urge to fidget, control distracting thoughts, and resist the temptation of falling asleep while patiently waiting in silent focus and stillness on a direct revelation of God.

In my experience, this is often what people think of contemplative prayer and because for many people sitting still without getting sleepy, jiggling about, or thinking about what has to be done tomorrow is almost impossible, they conclude it is not a spiritual practice for them. Contemplative prayer, therefore, has an image problem. I suffer from all these difficulties but find it a very accessible and practical form of prayer nonetheless. How that is possible probably comes down to how I define and approach contemplation and, by now, a lot of practice. Like a muscle strengthened with the repetition of exercise so too contemplative prayer becomes easier the more we do it.

Indeed, contemplative prayer has been the tool God has used

more than any other to shape me since 1997. Its role in my journey is crucial to the story I am sharing with you and I am passionate about its potential benefits for all of us. Therefore, I want to take the time to explain what I mean by contemplative prayer. I will come back to its implications for my own story in chapter four.

Let's start with the secular use of the word *contemplate* because it is familiar and anything we might say about the process of contemplation, as a matter of day to day use, remains true when we apply it to the realm of prayer. The primary difference between any secular or sacred use of the word is not the need for any odd, mystical, or mystifying practices but the presence of faith and the expectation that God is with us and will enliven our contemplation.

So what are we normally saying when we use the words *to contemplate*? What would you think I meant if I said I had walked up a mountain and contemplated the view once there? You would assume that I had done more than just glance at the view in passing. You would understand that I had taken time to savour and reflect at greater length on the view before me; that my observation of the view had been a thoughtful experience. You would also understand that, as the object of my contemplation, the view had **anchored** my attention and was at the root of any reflections flowing from it.

Contemplation is, therefore, quite simply what is happening when you **allow your attention to settle and to linger** gently on something. That something can be anything at all that you allowed to hold your attention; some aspect of creation, an object, a person, an event, a word and so on.

Contemplation is inevitably a **quiet process**. We are not speaking to the object of our contemplation; we are, in effect, **listening** to it and letting it speak to us in some way as we let it lead our response to it.

Contemplation, as a result, always has the potential to be **transformative**. Whenever we are so fully present to what holds our attention, we are affected by it in some way, however subtle its impact on us may be. It may be simply that, when we move on from our contemplation, we have a slightly deeper awareness or understanding of what we had been considering. Alternatively, we may have spotted something new that we had not realised before. However, it may be that the legacy of our contemplation is much more significant and results in some kind of change of heart or resolve to take action.

Let me take a specific example of a hilltop view to illustrate this contemplative process further. The picture below was taken at the top of a small hillside on the isle of Iona in Scotland.

If I simply look at this view, I take in its main physical elements of sky, cloud, land, rock, and sea. I also notice the houses and register that man is not just present but dwelling in this landscape as well.

I move from just seeing these things to contemplating them when I continue to linger and pay attention to them more deeply. There is no talking going on obviously; I am just quietly observing this picture. I am not distracted or struggling to stay focused because the picture has my attention well held. It also interests me to reflect further over it.

REFLECTION ON A HILLTOP VIEW

Before you read on, I would invite you to turn back to page 49 and to contemplate this hilltop view as well. Allow your gaze to linger on it. Be open and receptive to what it has to say to you. There are no specific insights you are trying to achieve. Simply allow the details of the picture to reveal it more fully to you. Also, don't worry if you feel that you see little more than I have already described. It may take some practice!

✠

My contemplation uncovers the following:

- 📖 the contrast between the mostly clear sky overhead and the quite dense bank of cloud in the distance
- 📖 the variations in light with patches of brilliance contrasting with more subdued tones
- 📖 the trails in the water suggesting currents or disturbance of some sort

- 📖 the inviting white sands at the edge of the island
- 📖 the trace of a road or track below the hill
- 📖 the rich green of the grass suggesting it is well watered by rain
- 📖 the different shapes of the stones with some well-rounded and others presenting sharp angular edges, and so on

This view is also speaking to me and moving me in a number of ways:

- 📖 I am experiencing its beauty and peacefulness which prompts delight and thankfulness in me.
- 📖 I feel a challenge arising from it as I reflect on humanity's footprint in this landscape. It is visible but limited and, I find, in harmony with what surrounds it. I am aware of a question this then puts to me about my own footprint and whether it is also in harmony with this world.
- 📖 The rocks speak to me too. Some appear like a solid pathway of stepping stones in a sea of grass whilst others have the potential to be hazards or obstacles to be navigated. I begin to wonder whether my pathway in life is solid or not. I consider whether I am currently facing any obstacles and, if I am, how I am choosing to navigate them. What or who is guiding me?

I have described above the fruit of my contemplation but the fruit of yours may be different. This landscape will speak to us in an individual way. However, we can share the expectation that, if we begin to pay attention to it, it will speak back to us. In so doing, it has the potential to leave us changed, transformed. This view changed me as its beauty uplifted and shared its peace with me. The questions it provoked also continue to challenge me.

None of the above was specifically prayer. However, the exact same process can become prayer. As already noted in chapter two, believing God is ever present throughout His Creation, as well as always with me by His Spirit, I can actively and expectantly seek that presence. I can look for Him as I pay attention to that which is before me; when I stop and linger, watching and listening for Him to speak to me out of the focus of my contemplation. This listening attitude is a fundamental attitude of all prayer as, even if we probably most often experience prayer as us talking to God, prayer actually begins with God having first reached out to interact with us.

If I bring a God-centred and prayerful focus to my contemplation of the hilltop view, allowing and expecting the Holy Spirit to be present, the process of gazing and listening does not change but the outcomes to some extent do:

> 📖 I may now experience the beauty and peacefulness of the landscape as gifts from God. My delight is in His creativity; an abundance that is so freely there for all of us to enjoy in His Creation. My thankfulness is directed to Him.

> 📖 I may feel the questions about my footprint in this world as potential challenges from God's Holy Spirit. This is God's world; we are stewards here and have a duty of care about how we dwell in it and move through it. Depending on how I assess my footprint, I might feel led to take some kind of action. This might be a matter for further prayer and reflection.

> 📖 As I consider the rocks, scriptures may come to mind which encourage me to make God the strong foundation

on which I stand; to make Jesus the one I follow so that
I do remain on solid ground and navigate safely the
hazards life holds.

The outcomes of your contemplation of this hilltop view, which
may have been different to mine, would similarly reflect God's
presence with you in your contemplation, if approached as prayer.

The mystery of contemplative prayer does not lie in any special
process, but in the constant inexplicable wonder that God is so
very close and present to us all the time, if only we had the eyes
to see and the ears to hear Him. The words of the psalmist express
this better than I can:

Psalm 8:3–4

When I consider your heavens,
  the work of your fingers,
the moon and the stars,
  which you have set in place,
what is mankind that you are mindful of them,
  human beings that you care for them?

The psalmist took in the vast canopy of the night sky and God
spoke to him. He felt the extraordinary juxtaposition of the
sweeping breadth of Creation, with all the power behind it, and the
gentle tenderness of a God who bends down over His Creation to
engage intimately with it; to have concern for the psalmist, to have
concern for you and concern for me. There is transformation here.
The psalmist's contemplation has led to something deeper than just
head knowledge. One senses that this experience has reverberated

within his soul as well, for in that star studded sky, the wonder of God has been more fully revealed to him.

> **REFLECTION: THE WONDER OF GOD**
>
> If you have memories of experiencing God through His Creation, take a moment to recollect one such experience so you can savour and enjoy what it revealed again.
>
> ✠

It is probably easy to see how bringing a prayerful gaze to Creation might reveal God. However, if you think back to my reflection on the spoon, this too could have been contemplative prayer. The focus of my attention was a machine-made object, but the spoon nevertheless spoke to me about itself and prompted questions. In prayer, I would have been listening for the Spirit's prompting in that process. If I was to reflect prayerfully on the spoon again now, I might find there is nothing new in my reflections. Alternatively, I might notice some thoughts have a greater shimmer to them – they stand out more than the others – suggesting that I linger there and listen further.

I said earlier that when we use the word *contemplate* in a secular context, we can apply it to contemplating anything at all and the same is no less true in the context of contemplative prayer. All aspects and elements of life can be prayed over contemplatively and the basic process is the same – we stop and we linger, we let the focus of our attention speak to us, and thereby we are open to its potential to transform us. The difference, once again, is only in God's presence and our seeking of Him.

Our daily lives, therefore, are rich with the potential to reveal God's transformative presence. God is through all of His Creation and He dwells with us by His Holy Spirit; every moment is, therefore, as full of that which is holy as it is that which is secular. We can miss God's presence not because it is withheld but because we are not expecting it or because we are so busy and rushed that we do not have the time – the gap between breath and breath†– to listen out for and notice Him revealed within even the most ordinary moments of our day.

Moses comes to mind again at this point. I wonder how easy it might have been for him to ignore that burning bush. We will never know, because we know that he didn't ignore it; it intrigued him and he heeded its 'call'. I think Moses then contemplated that burning bush. He had a long, lingering look at it and, in the process, God revealed He was the explanation for it; the presence that is all consuming and burns on through the present without burning up. Moses did not have to be sitting in an empty room avoiding distractions and fighting off the urge to scratch the end of his nose to have this direct experience of the divine. It happened right in the middle of his day as the sheep roamed.

This experience of Moses could be seen as a practical example of one expression of what it might mean to *pray continually* as Scripture encourages us to.* Very few of us would be able to create all day the silence we normally associate with prayer. Our lives are full of commitments and responsibilities that bring noise and

---

†I deliberately use the word gap again here to recall the gaps, however small, that exist between the inhaled and exhaled breaths and which we can think of as the dwelling place of God in each breath. Again, see page 31.

*See 1 Thessalonians 5: 16–18.

clamour, rather than peace and quiet. Nevertheless, we might find that we have the opportunity to praise God or to pray for specific needs, or to meditate on his Word because, although our hands may be occupied, our minds may not be. However, sometimes we are taken up in something that does not leave such space. In those instances, how can we possibly pray *continually* unless our understanding of prayer also includes the option of an attentive and open heart, which through all that is happening or being said, is simply ever alert for and listening out for God?

His voice may be the merest whisper and easily missed if we do not have an ear out for it. His presence may be overlooked if we are not expectant of it. Perhaps it is the object in our hands or the words of a neighbour, the birdsong or the bare trees in the garden that will be the vehicle for God's word to us and our further transformation. Alternatively, it may be the mess in the kitchen, a situation at work, the joy running through a celebration, the novel we are reading, the music we are listening to, or a world event that will point to His presence. He could speak out of any aspect of our lives which makes every day full of potential revelation and very exciting.

If contemplation were a muscle, we would notice that it gets its biggest workout through the warp and weft of our days as we learn to be alert for God. However, even with the best intentions, our lives can sometimes drown out an awareness of God's voice and presence in the moment that we might, however, pick up if we took the time to review our day. As a result, it is worthwhile to set aside time regularly to look back in search of where God might have been. Therefore, I have outlined in Appendix 2 how to approach this type of contemplation of our daily lives.

We are urged to pray continually but being intentional about prayer is important; whatever the form of our prayer whether adoration, confession, thanksgiving, supplication, contemplation, or other. We can benefit from specifically setting aside time to draw near to God.

In the context of contemplation, if not doing so to review one's day, we might do so with the intent to focus on God or to contemplate his Word in greater depth.

Practical examples of these types of prayerful contemplation, therefore, would be helpful. To that end, how we might approach the contemplation of God is outlined in detail in Appendix 3. Referring you to the appendices for this and the contemplation of our daily lives is not meant to suggest that they are in some way unimportant, but simply that the level of detail in which they are covered is not needed at this point in the narrative.

By contrast, it will be helpful if I demonstrate now how the basic principles of contemplation apply when it comes to Scripture, as there will be opportunities in future chapters for you to have a go at this type of contemplation.

The contemplation of Scripture is, in essence, no different to the contemplative process already described; we give our attention to a scene depicted in Scripture and allow it to speak to us. However, we probably do not have the benefit of photography or cinematography to lay out the specifics of that scene visually. Our contemplation is, therefore, an imaginative process; one for which we use the inner eye, but one that is nonetheless anchored in the text before us, keeping us alert and focused.

Not all of Scripture lends itself easily to this contemplative gaze as sometimes there is no scene as such to be observed. These texts can invite our meditation instead, as we ruminate on their meaning.[†] However, those texts which tell a story, such as the gospels, are ideal for contemplation.

I find it most helpful to work with fairly short segments of narrative text. However, that is only a suggestion not a rule; allow God to guide what you do. In other words, if you feel the Holy Spirit guiding you to stop and focus on one small part of a story, do follow and trust that prompting. The aim is not to finish the text but to let God lead you and speak to you through it as He determines. You can always contemplate the longer text again another time.

Indeed, praying with Scripture contemplatively can move you in many ways. You may be struck by specific words; words which could offer comfort and strength or could challenge and disturb you. You may have a sense of being drawn closer to God as you experience perhaps His love, joy, hope, or peace. You might also feel moved to action. Whatever your response, when you are aware of being moved or stirred, do not rush on, rather linger over that touch of God's Word so you can fully receive from it.

In such instances, it can also be tempting to start analysing what is happening mid-contemplation. However, trying to understand how God is working in you is best done afterwards. When you have finished praying, you step back from the experience and consider it as a whole with a view to discerning how God was present in it.

Let's consider, as a practical example of the process, how you might approach the contemplation of **John 1:35–39**.

[†]See Appendix 7, Frequently Asked Questions, for an explanation of the difference I draw between meditation and contemplation.

Step 1: Centring

I would begin my time of contemplation by finding a quiet and solitary space away from that which would otherwise easily distract me. I would then take some time to relax and settle in that space. I am seeking to be comfortable in my posture but alert and to become more fully present to that moment by letting go of what I have been doing previously or may be looking to do later.

A helpful technique for letting go of distractions and becoming more attentive in prayer is to focus on my breathing for a short while. I notice its rhythm and, in particular, the transitions between inhalation, exhalation, and back. I accentuate the movement by breathing slower and deeper. I do this ten or so times keeping my focus throughout on my breath.[†]

However, if other thoughts do come to mind as I do this, I give them a nod, so to speak, but gently set them aside or write them down if they matter and I do not want to forget them. I will make sure I have some paper and a pen to hand for this. Then I will return my attention to my breathing.

As I breathe deeply in this way, I allow my body to relax into the seat on which I am sitting. In effect, I let the chair fully hold my weight; I do not try to hold myself rather I let the chair do the work. I am not slumping in the chair, as good erect posture helps me to remain alert, but I trust the chair to bear my weight. This gives physical expression to the trust I am expressing in prayer that it is God who truly holds me in being. Starting my prayer time in this way is often referred to as '**Centring**'.

As I centre myself in the present moment by focusing on my

[†]We have already had a go at this – see page 31.

breathing, I may also, after a while, take a word or simple phrase which I will slowly repeat as I continue to focus on the movement of my breath. The repetition of a word not only helps me to stay focused but also, if my mind has wandered, taking up the word and repeating it again, helps me to return to focus more easily and quickly. There are no specific right words to choose in this instance. My choice of word or words will vary. I might settle on the repetition of the prayer known as the Jesus Prayer: 'Lord Jesus Christ, Son of God, have mercy on me, a sinner' or perhaps words like 'Come Holy Spirit, come' or single words that might express a grace that I would seek from God at that moment such as 'Joy', 'Love', 'Hope', 'Wisdom', and so on.

Step 2: Read the Passage at Least Twice

When I feel settled, I read slowly through the text two or three times allowing the narrative and any dialogue to sink in.

John 1:35–39

The next day John was there again with two of his disciples. When he saw Jesus passing by, he said, "Look, the Lamb of God!"

When the two disciples heard him say this, they followed Jesus. Turning around, Jesus saw them following and asked, "What do you want?"

They said, "Rabbi" (which means "Teacher"), "where are you staying?"

"Come," he replied, "and you will see."

So they went and saw where he was staying, and they spent that day with him. It was about four in the afternoon.

Step 3: Contemplation of the Passage

The invitation then is to enter into this story by setting the scene and experiencing what is happening from the perspective of one of the characters. I choose who I will be: perhaps John, or one of the two disciples, or a passing observer or even Jesus himself.

There is no one right way for me to set the scene. However, there are some clues earlier in the chapter that are helpful. We are told that John the Baptist is at Bethany on the other side of the Jordan. Therefore, I know to set this scene in or near a town with a river flowing nearby. My imagined depiction does not have to be correct in some literal sense; I do not need to know what the Jordan or Bethany looked like at the time to imagine the river or town in a meaningful way.

In setting the scene as fully as I can, I imagine:

- the setting itself: the backdrop of the town, the river, the road Jesus is 'passing by' on, the daytime light
- the ambient sounds: voices, running water, feet crunching over stone
- the touch of the environment: the hard road beneath my feet, the dust between my toes, the heat on my brow
- all the little details which are given or alluded to that we so easily skip over

I then relive the depicted scene from my chosen perspective within the narrative. I hear the words being spoken whether they are being said to me or whether I am, in the story, overhearing them being said to someone else. I remember to take my time allowing God's Spirit to guide the pace and length of what I do.

Step 4: Review

When I have finished praying, I take a bit longer to reflect over what I have experienced. I notice again, especially, where I might have felt God stir me in response to His Word. Questions that can be helpful as you do this include ones like the following:

- 📖 What, if anything, particularly struck me?
- 📖 How did I feel? What might these feelings be saying to me?
- 📖 How am I more aware of God's presence?
- 📖 Is there anything to which it would be helpful to return next time I pray?

I also take time to discern whether what I think I have heard is of God. Not every thought that we may have is automatically of God even in prayer. There are practical suggestions for how to approach this question of discernment in Appendix 7 which addresses this and other frequently asked questions.

Step 5: Journal

I make a note of the insights or questions which arise from the prayer time in a journal. These notes provide me with a helpful record of how God is working in and present with me which I can look back over and learn from as time goes on.

Finally, I am as honest as I can be as I journal. What I have written is for my eyes only unless I decide otherwise.

✠

WHAT DO YOU WANT?

If you would like to have a go at contemplating John 1: 35–39 either now or later, you can do so following the process just outlined on pages 59 to 62.

Alternatively, you will find another guided example, a contemplation of The Woman at the Well, in Appendix 4.

The process outlined may feel at first quite complicated but with practice the suggested steps become familiar, and don't really feel like steps in a process at all.

Indeed, as I said at the start of the chapter, contemplative prayer is a label, albeit one that can seem off-putting and alienating at first. However, whatever the focus of our contemplation, contemplative prayer is really just shorthand for what is happening when we hear (Stop), respond (Look), and are transformed (Listen) by God's invitation to –

Psalm 46:10

Be still and know that I am God.

Chapter 4

My Soul Finds Rest in God

Stillness and quiet have descended over the room as we all sit contemplating John 1:35–39. I am following Jesus along the road when He turns and asks me, 'What do you want?'

This passage, which we took as an example in chapter three, was also my introduction to the contemplation of Scripture over the retreat weekend in 1997. The retreat leader had read the passage to us several times before guiding us through it very slowly. She had allowed us time to picture the scene, to enter into its narrative, and she had emphasised this question, '**What do you want?**' inviting us to respond with our deepest desire.

What did I want from Jesus?

I had already expressed some hopes and desires for the weekend before I did this contemplation, but I had approached these like a set of aims.† They were the result of engaging my mind rather than also being the deeper response of my heart and soul. It is not that they were divorced from my answer to the question for they remained relevant, but nor did they capture my actual response.

In my contemplation, when Jesus had turned round, I had instinctively pictured Him holding out His hand to me as He asked

---

†See page 41.

me, "What do you want?" Being offered His hand, I had taken it and, in doing so, I had an overwhelming feeling of wanting to know every detail of it. I wanted to trace the lines, to feel the carpenter's callouses, to know its strength, its gentleness, and its goodness. What did I want? I desperately wanted to know Him better; more intimately.

My desire was not for something other than God but for God Himself. This does not make me super-spiritual; it reveals a truth about all of us. Whether we know it or not, we long for home. We long for the One who has always known us and longs for us as well; who calls us His beloved children and invites us to call Him Abba, Father. God desires that we should know this with every fibre of our being: body, mind and soul. As a result, His Holy Spirit works in us shaping our desires for a deeper relationship with Him.[†]

Uncovering such deep desire in me was profoundly moving for me at the time. I was startled by the measure of longing that I felt. However, I was also comforted and encouraged by what I realised was a promise as well as an invitation in the response of Jesus. I knew that if I followed Jesus when He said, 'Come and you will see' and if I 'spent that day with Him', He would indeed reveal Himself more fully to me.

The contemplation lasted about twenty minutes. Therefore, although I heard His invitation, 'spending the day with Him' was never intended or going to happen in a literal manner. Anyway there was far too much bubbling to the surface to be addressed and resolved in one contemplative sitting. The retreat weekend was

---

[†]See Hebrews 11:13 –16; Psalm 139:13–16, Luke 15:20, and Galatians 4:6–7.

unfolding for me like a small earthquake with each tremor causing fractures in my personal landscape.

The first tremor was the disquiet I had arrived with about the busyness of my days. This was brought into sharper focus that weekend. I had to get to grips with what was motivating all the activity as well as working out what to carry on versus what to let go.

The latter was true not least because of the second tremor which was the repetition and lingering echo of the words, 'God is good'. I was so profoundly struck by them; I understood that I needed to stay with them so God could reveal more fully why they mattered. The dissonance I felt between my head knowledge of God's goodness and my actions, which were rooted in my heart, needed to be explored.

This linked in turn to the third tremor: the recognition that I was thirsty and longing for a more intimate relationship with God; one which flowed from *both* the inner knowing of the heart and the intellectual knowing and acceptance of the head. Like David in Psalm 62, I longed to be able to say that my soul found rest in God.

The result of all these tremors though was not random devastation so much as the opening up of that soil in which God clearly intended to work in a new and deeper way: my heart.

However, although I came away from that weekend in February 1997 confident that God was moving in me and inviting me to move with Him to address my tiredness, discover His goodness, and satisfy my thirst, I did not feel led to make any immediate big changes. It is not that I was doing nothing. I was waiting; paying close attention especially to what my life and God's Word might reveal about specific next steps.

As I contemplated regularly my activities and relationships, I was able to discern God confirming the messages in the tremors from the retreat as well as uncovering new insights.[†] For example, over the Easter holidays that year, as a family we attended a week-long Christian event at which the most repeated song was 'God is good, all the time' by Don Moen. This song spoke directly to my feeling that I had to explore how that was true generally about God as well as specifically in my own life.

If I had easily enough identified that the sheer volume of what I was doing was a problem, it was harder to admit, but nevertheless becoming clear, that there were also some relationships that required addressing. These were interactions based on a need in me to fix things for others that actually were not for me to fix. However, instead of being overcome by a sense of hopelessness before all that needed to change in and around me, I was gradually being lifted by the thought that what I could not do, Jesus ultimately could. God is good.

The contemplation of Scripture was particularly helpful as the year progressed. Reflecting in May on Jesus washing the feet of the disciples at the last supper, I pictured Jesus gently cleaning my feet.[*] When He was done, I felt He was saying to me, 'When you are with me, I want you to rest'. In the contemplation, as I imagined it at the time, I wanted to get up and serve. After all, isn't that what this passage is about? Isn't Jesus modelling for us

---

[†]I did this by contemplating my daily life using the approach outlined in Appendix 2.
[*]John 13:1–5.

how we must serve one another? However, I sensed Him gently pressing me back into my seat saying, 'No, you must rest, you can serve later. Rest now, in prayer you must rest with me. You must accept that I want to love you, care for you, and tender to you'. An invitation which chimed with other words I had written in my journal too: 'I feel I must accept and receive Christ rather than work myself ragged for Him. Accept His grace and love for me'.

Was I working for my salvation? I knew I couldn't. Our salvation comes through faith alone.[†] It is grace all the way. I knew that. However, I also knew that works matter. In James 2:17 we read, 'faith by itself, if it is not accompanied by action, is dead' because works bear witness to and give expression to a living faith. Paul also tells us we must 'work out' our salvation.[*]

I was not confused by these verses. However, I was beginning to realise yet again that whatever I knew with my head about salvation, my actions, uncovering what lay in my heart, suggested I might nonetheless be working for it.

As I reflected on why that might be I was aware that I had soaked up the world's message that we are most loveable for what we are: for our looks, our successes, our achievements, our merits, call it what you will, let's call it our works. Also, the devil is exceptionally wily. What better way to bind up one of God's children than in the shiny mantle of holy works?

In discerning which insights might be of God and which might not be, I was helped by a Spiritual Director, whom I had started seeing monthly soon after the retreat. A Spiritual Director is

---

[†]See Ephesians 2:8–9.

[*]See Philippians 2:12.

someone who meets with you regularly and, seeking the Holy Spirit's guidance, undertakes to listen with you for how God's voice is being revealed in your life, in your reading of Scripture, and in your times of prayer.[†]

In the process of talking about our lives, our spiritual journey, and our experience of God, all sorts of things can emerge. Our image of God is exposed with its truth and its distortions, our fears and hopes are both drawn into the light, our motivations and our temptations are revealed, and so on. Spiritual Direction inevitably, therefore, depends on trust of the other and the work of God's Holy Spirit to be most effective.

A Spiritual Director is not there to tell you what to do. They may ask questions, they may make suggestions for prayer and bible reading, they may offer a helpful insight or reflect back what they have heard, and explore for how God is or is not present in that with you. What they will always do is leave you free and encourage you to grow and deepen your relationship with God in response to His invitation to you.

There is a particular contemplation that I did around this time which highlights how a Spiritual Director can be helpful. I had been contemplating the story of Zacchaeus, the tax collector, who, because he is a short man, climbs a tree in order to catch a glimpse of Jesus who is passing that way. Jesus sees him and tells Zacchaeus to come down as He will be staying at his house that

---

[†]A Spiritual Director is by no means essential for the Christian journey. However, I have found great blessing from having such a companion especially when it comes to helping with discernment. I would not hesitate to recommend looking for one. However, it does have to be the right relationship for both parties. Therefore, it is worth approaching on a trial basis of maybe three or so months with the understanding that one or both might conclude the relationship is not quite working and with the associated freedom not to take it further.

day. A request Zacchaeus gladly responds to.[†]

Although I pictured myself in the place of the tax collector in the story, I decided not to climb a tree. This was not because I am tall but rather because I have always been reasonably good at getting people's attention if I want it. I decided I could get the attention of Jesus without having to climb a tree if I wanted to.

When I was discussing this passage with my Spiritual Director, she highlighted the hidden implication of what I had shared with her: if I need to get the attention of Jesus then that is because I do not already have it. Whereas the truth is I always have the attention of Jesus.

REFLECTION

Take a few minutes to consider this simple but profound truth: you always have the attention of Jesus.

✠

This suggested another question and potential insight about all my activity at the time. Was I so busy because I was actually trying to get the attention of Jesus rather than trusting that I had His attention already?

I had no awareness of this implication of thinking 'if I need the attention of Jesus, I know I could get it'. Sometimes we cannot see for ourselves what is revealed in plain sight. We need a companion who will listen and hear within our words what we cannot discern for ourselves.

[†]See Luke 19:1–10.

As the year advanced, insights continued to be given. However, I was still unclear about specific next steps which might lead to changes in what I was actually doing. Therefore, a second retreat in the autumn provided a welcome opportunity to focus my listening further on what those steps might be. This was a week-long retreat in daily life which suggested contemplation as the primary method for prayer and Spiritual Direction as the means to review that prayer time.

The retreat began on day one with everyone together but, thereafter, the commitment was to make time on our own within the normal run of each day to pray for half an hour. We were also to meet with a Spiritual Director for half an hour daily to review its outcomes.

At the first meeting, to help us get started, we were offered a number of different bible verses from which we could choose one to contemplate. One of the options was based on a verse in Hosea 2:

I will lead her into the desert and speak to her heart.[†]

I knew this was the starting point for me. It spoke clearly to the longing I had been carrying all year to know Jesus more intimately from the heart and not just the head. This verse also gave me a clear indication of how God might actually speak to my heart: in a place set apart, in the solitude of the desert.

---

†This wording is based on Hosea 2:16
'But look, I am going to seduce her and lead her into the desert and speak to her heart'
(NJB)

REFLECTION ON THE DESERT

What does the desert say to you?

✠

I focused my contemplation that evening on the desert. I pictured a landscape which was harsh, arid, silent, inhospitable, and exposed; a place that offered nowhere to hide and left you vulnerable. These attributes of the desert, ones which could be expected to deter, I realised were key. I wrote in my journal that same evening that I wanted to 'cease resisting being vulnerable' to God. The desert offered itself as a natural place for this to happen. It was, though, a dangerous place to go alone. In the desert I would need a guide; one I could trust to lead and guard me whilst there and who afterwards could guide me safely back.

However, over the week that followed, and as I contemplated a variety of other bible passages, it became apparent that, if I resisted being vulnerable to God, it was because of a lack of trust. It was not that I consciously and knowingly chose to distrust God but the choices I made revealed that I trusted myself more. I felt safest when I was in control or, of course, thought I was. This was the coping mechanism I had first adopted when much younger to manage my fears and vulnerability in the face of change or challenge. By 1997, it was also a hard-to-kick habit.

Trust only grows slowly. It takes root as we begin to perceive that someone is trustworthy; that they are true to their word or reliable in their actions. It is no different with God. If we are aware of God's love in practical ways in our lives, if we experience His mercy and goodness, it will be easier to surrender to Him. Our trust will have developed a solid base in our experience. It is not for nothing that God repeatedly tells the Israelites to remember the Exodus and their deliverance. Remembering His faithfulness and goodness to them would keep them faithful to Him because they would know they could trust Him.

This also draws into focus one of the great benefits of being attentive for God's presence through each day as we review our days in prayer. The more we notice God is with us, as He promises, capturing the blessings then revealed, the more we will be prepared to trust Him in all circumstances.[†]

I anticipated that deeper trust would be a fruit of the desert experience with God, yet I needed trust to get started, and I lacked it. It felt like I was trying to put the cart before the horse. However, although I lacked the immediate trust necessary to be easily vulnerable to God, like with any lack, we can ask God to

---

[†]See Appendix 2, Contemplating our Daily Lives.

give us by grace what we cannot do for ourselves.

This links again to desire. I desperately wanted God to speak to my heart; this would happen in the desert and, therefore, I also wanted to trust God so that I could go to such a vulnerable and challenging place with Him. God will work with what we can offer Him, which includes our desire where He is present.

Wanting to trust God, I asked for the grace of trust. Trust did not blossom and fruit in me overnight because I had done so but, as I prayed for it, I became alert for signs of God's presence and blessing.

Praying contemplatively with Scripture was particularly enabling me to draw closer to God in trust. As I used the mind's eye to set the scenes and to enter into them, I was beginning to picture Jesus in ways that made His presence more immediate and real to me. Praying on one occasion with Psalm 23, for example, I imagined being with Jesus, the Shepherd, in a beautiful mountain valley and being taken to a high pasture where we sat down in the sunshine together by a stream of water.

Psalm 23:1–4

The Lord is my shepherd, I lack nothing.
He makes me lie down in green pastures,
he leads me beside quiet waters,
he refreshes my soul.
He guides me along the right paths
for his name's sake.
Even though I walk
through the darkest valley,

I will fear no evil,
  for you are with me;
your rod and your staff,
    they comfort me.

As I listened with the mind's ear, I heard the running water and beyond it birdsong. I felt at rest and a deep sense of security and peace. The place itself contributed to this feeling of comfort and wellbeing but, more importantly, the presence of Jesus did so. I pondered afterwards in my journal how I might 'gaze on the beauty of the Lord' in this way all the time.[†]

I also wrote that I could not imagine this valley in shadow with Jesus present. It was not to deny the reality of hard and dark times in our lives, occasions when we might even have no sense of God, but to recognise the transformative potential of Jesus when we were confident of His presence. There was great comfort and hope in this realisation. Small and tender shoots of trust began to take root, enough for me to get started.

REFLECTION ON TRUST

There are two gospel stories which might come to mind in the context of trust. The story of Jesus and Peter walking on water in Matthew 14:22–33 and the calming of the storm in Mark 4:35–41.

[†]Psalm 27:4

76

I would invite you to choose one of these stories to contemplate. If you are aware that trust is also difficult for you, then do ask God, as you begin, to give you the grace of trust.

Step 1: Centring

Begin by taking some time to centre yourself by focusing on your breathing and/or a phrase or key word such as *Trust.*

✠

Step 2: Read the Passage at Least Twice

✠

Step 3: Contemplation of the Passage

Set the scene in your mind's eye and live into the story from your chosen perspective as one of the characters in the story.

✠

Step 4: Review

Take some time to **review** your contemplation when you have finished. Notice any particular words, feelings or responses that spoke to you or struck you and point perhaps to the Holy Spirit's prompting.

✠

Step 5: Journal

Finally, keep a record in your **journal** of what you have uncovered and experienced.

✠

My Spiritual Director knew that I would need a map and a guide in the desert and she had both for me. In the 16th century, St Ignatius of Loyola had developed a series of exercises that encouraged and helped those who did them to deepen their relationship with God. These exercises were, and still are, done as a long retreat either over a concentrated thirty day period or, as I was to do them, in daily life, taking the time necessary to complete them amidst the other demands of one's days.

If done in thirty days, each day the retreatant spends six hours in silent prayer as they contemplate and/or meditate over the Exercise for the day. In the seventh hour they meet with a Spiritual Director to discuss the time of prayer.

When done in daily life, each day would usually correspond to a week. Instead of praying for six hours each day, the retreatant undertakes to pray for an hour each day over six days and, on the seventh day of the week, to meet with a Spiritual Director to discuss those prayer times as a whole. As a result, when undertaken in daily life, the retreat will take at least 30 weeks and often longer allowing for holidays and unforeseen events.

The Exercises, based on the 30 day model, break down into four approximately week-long periods:

📖 Week 1 is spent looking at our sinfulness and need of God

📖 Week 2 looks at the life of Christ

📖 Week 3 reflects on the death of Christ and finally

📖 Week 4 focuses on the resurrection of Christ

REFLECTION: STEPPING OUT

Another contemplation which can be helpful for exploring how we trust God and how we approach, more generally, our Christian journey is one which needs to be done with a partner.

Taking it in turns, one of you is blindfolded and allows the other to guide them through a space listening only to their voice and prompting touch.

Before you begin, the guide makes clear the destination within the space but not the route that will be taken to get there.

When you have reached the destination, swap roles and do it again. The destination can be the same but not the route.

When you have both had a go, take some time separately to review how it felt. Notice, in particular, how comfortable or easy it was – or not – to trust the guide. Also, reflect on whether, knowing the destination, you were able to step attentively through each *present* moment listening to the voice of the one-who-walks-with-us without trying to second-guess or anticipate the route.

✠

Heading to the desert, even in the form of a retreat in daily life, begged the question of how I was going to add another major commitment to what I was already doing.

The answer was not to make it something more and extra but

to approach it as the retreat it was, stepping back, therefore, from my other activities for its duration. This was not a step to be taken lightly even though I was certain of the calling. As a result, I took the final months of that year to prepare the way ahead with a view to starting the retreat in the January of 1998.

On a spiritual level, this period of preparation included a programme of prayer specifically focused on recognising God's love for me. Over four or five weeks, I contemplated scriptures that particularly emphasised God's overwhelming compassion and care for me. This was intended as a sound and necessary foundation from which to head subsequently into the first period of the Exercises which focuses on sin. It is important to know at all times that God's love is greater than our sinfulness. Appreciating God's love for me further strengthened my tender shoots of trust as well.

On a practical level, the actual process of letting go began; I had the necessary conversations to enable me to retreat from my activities. Although most people were supportive, some were flummoxed. A prolonged break to head off on a personal journey, even if it is with Jesus, can sound like navel-gazing self-indulgence and to some it did.

It is not that there was any active ill-will rather, those who questioned it, could not see in me the need I knew existed. The idea, for example, that I might be empty was hard for some to recognise because I was good at hiding just how depleted I was. However, there is nothing wrong with challenging questions; the peace I felt as I explained myself was an added confirmation that this was the right decision.

I gave up everything.

Actually that is not true. It is what I want to write, for it was what

I felt God called me to do. The fact is I didn't give up everything. When it had come to giving up the Church Board, a committee which met only once every six weeks, the chairperson's response had been along the lines of '*Surely* not the Board as well! We hardly meet. Why would you need to give up the Board as well?'

Having been released from all my other activities and caring what others thought of me, I was unable and unwilling to insist and so I let myself be persuaded to continue. I remained on the Board for a quiet life even though a quiet life does not ring the same soul note as peace. I also carried on because I was afraid of being thought utterly self-centred and not because God was asking me to. I would begin this retreat as I was, not as I might wish to be.

The year 1997 with all its tremors, waiting, and discoveries finally concluded. We were still deep in the Scottish winter with its low winter light and short days when I stepped into January 1998 and the bright exposing light of the desert. I was not afraid of what might happen in that wilderness. I believed God was with me and would provide the bread and life-giving waters that would sustain me. Also, as anyone who has seen rain fall in the desert will know, when water flows, the desert blooms and is transformed into a place of beauty and hope.

Chapter 5

I Will Lead Her Into The Desert and Speak To Her Heart

I spent eighteen months in my spiritual desert with Jesus.

When we weren't exploring rocky outcrops with wide views or treading the way in narrow valleys, we camped out much of the time by an oasis in the shade of tall palms and dates trees – or so I imagined it. Our encounters could at times be incredibly challenging but they always drew me closer, unfolding for me God's love, mercy, and compassion in ever clearer ways. They developed in me an ever increasing appreciation of who He was as Creator and Saviour. I also gained greater self-awareness perceiving my brokenness and my sinfulness with a clarity which would have been overwhelming had it not been that Jesus did not uncover my frailty to punish or depress me but to set me free.

The retreat has been of lasting benefit to me in too many ways to share them all and in more ways than are relevant here. However, there were some outcomes from the retreat that I think were not only personal but can speak to all of us.

Firstly, the **practice of contemplation** became familiar and with it came an increasing appreciation of its value as a discipline. I won't claim to have prayed for an hour a day every day over the eighteen months but I entered into the retreat experience as faithfully as I could. The contemplation of Scripture being a significant part of the process, my experience of praying in this way developed rapidly.

The retreat encouraged me to be alert for echoes of those prayer times in the lived experience of my day as well. I was especially aware of this when, at night, I would look back with a contemplative gaze over my day. It was often amazing how my broader experiences that day related to the retreat material I had in hand thus enabling any revelations from the latter to be taken even deeper. The expectation of finding God in all things started to take root. My daily walk has been more attentive, and therefore contemplative, ever since.†

The retreat also uncovered for me **the benefits of solitude**. Solitude is not loneliness. These are two very different experiences. When lonely, you are bereft of company you would otherwise desire. You are in lack. However, in solitude you seek God's presence. You are not alone, you are not without; you are with God.

In solitude, you can meditate and contemplate Scripture, you can speak and listen to God; you can be open and most truly yourself. In solitude, God can be ministering to you as you need. He can refresh and renew you, comfort and encourage you, convict and admonish you, teach and guide you; He can root you in His love and transform you.

We can carve out and safeguard time for solitude; a quiet time when we read Scripture and/or pray. However, we may also find solitude at other unplanned times; perhaps when we listen to music, go for a walk, have a bath/shower, do the chores or go for a drive.

---

†See Appendix 2, Contemplating my Daily Life.

Prior to heading into the desert, when I was so over-stretched, I was empty partly because I did not have enough time in solitude. I missed out, as a result, on the opportunity it could have offered me both to be renewed by God and to receive the wisdom I needed about investing in or curtailing my activities.

Solitude and community, however, are not at odds with each other; they belong together. The movement of a pendulum can help us to understand how this is so. As it swings to and fro marking out each second, we can also imagine it beating a pulse between the secular and the sacred. Every moment is thus full of the world and full of God.

In our own lives we need to find that rhythm of moving out towards others and back towards God; one taking us towards community, the other taking us towards solitude. We need this swing towards solitude to be resourced by God, so that what we receive from God is what we take out towards the world. We might be reminded again of our breath – the inhalation being the inward movement towards God and the exhalation being our outward movement towards the world.

The retreat also encouraged me **to pray continually** by being attentive for God's voice whether I was specifically taking time apart to that end or not. As a result, I discovered that, personally, I was most sensitive to the timbre of God's voice when I was walking amidst His Creation.

I live in a coastal town with the North Sea to the east and low rising hills to the west. Two rivers cut down towards the sea on either side of the town with woodland or farm and parkland along much of their routes. There is all the wildlife you would expect in such a landscape. I cannot step outside my front door without being immeasurably blessed by the beauty of this place and the message it holds about the creativity of our God and His interest in our extraordinary world. This never fails to lift me, to encourage me, to inspire me, and to give me hope. I find all sorts of spiritual pictures revealed in what I am seeing as well.

For example, when I see the snowdrops breaking through the cold hard ground, even as winter still holds the land in its grip, I hear messages about joy and resilience. I hear the truth that joy can break forth in the midst of our distress. When I spotted these particular snowdrops hemmed in and under attack on every side, I heard the promise that, even when we are being overwhelmed by our circumstances, the God-who-is-with-us can nonetheless enable us to grow and shine forth.

Creation speaks powerfully to me and perhaps you find it does to you too. Or maybe you hear God's voice more readily in music, art or some other pursuit that speaks to your heart. We are all different. God knows that and can take account of that in how He approaches us.

REFLECTION ON HEARING GOD'S VOICE

Are you aware of being more sensitive to God's voice in one way rather than another or at certain times rather than others?

If not, take some time to contemplate your life with a view to uncovering whether there is any pattern to how and when you hear God's voice most clearly. One way to get behind this question might be to consider when you feel most alive? Where is your attention most naturally given? Ask the Holy Spirit to show you and to remind you again of times when you recognised His voice.

✠

If you do not discern an answer now then I would encourage you to remain attentive for one over the days and weeks to come. Be alert for times when you feel aware of God's presence; sensitive to His voice.

If you do know the answer to this question then you might like to make time now for God in that simple way. If Creation speaks powerfully to you – and weather and health allow you to – take a walk outside or else imagine a favourite walk. If it is music, then listen to something you love. If it is art or poetry, sport or anything else then pick up your paintbrush, your pen, your book, your kit, or whatever you need and be with God in it attentive to what He might say through it.

✠

Another insight, which I uncovered as I not only reviewed the day past for God's presence but also took time to look back for Him over the broader sweep of my life journey, was that **God does not come once but again and again as Saviour and Redeemer** in our lives whether we have the wit to ask for His help or not.

For example, the move between Canada and Argentina had been a very difficult one for me. I had moved from a Canadian high school to a French lycée, changing school systems as I did so. In the process, I slid from a very comfortable position towards the top of my class to the bottom. A spot with which I was unfamiliar – I committed a lot of nervous energy to getting out of it again as quickly as possible.

It was not just the different school curriculum that had caused this. I had gone from speaking English most of the time to having to speak French most of the time; a language I knew relatively well but, initially, not fluently. I also had to do a significant portion of my lessons in Spanish which, on arrival, I did not speak at all. Add in other cultural changes, having to make new friends, and the growing pains of adolescence, and these years were shot through with constant stress and challenge.

However, these were not unhappy years. I had become a Christian just two years before and, although my faith was still very new with only the tiniest of roots, it nonetheless made a difference during this period. I always knew, if nothing else, that there was someone much bigger than me who was on my side. It was a reference point that kept things in some kind of perspective. It was, though, only as I looked back with Jesus by my side in the desert, that I realised just how important my relationship with God had been during my teenage years. I was twenty years late with my thank you, but I did feel tremendous gratitude for what I could see was not just the saving of my soul at one point in time, but the daily saving that God performs in our lives, as He strengthens and equips us to live in the midst of any and all our circumstances.

The heart knowledge I gained from remembering this and other times when God's saving love had touched my life was that God was indeed good. He never ceases to reach out and to call us beloved.

This is no less true when we are off track and have gone astray; at such times we need to remember these words:

Romans 5:8

But God demonstrates his own love for us in this: While we were still sinners, Christ died for us.

We may not think we deserve to be rescued but nothing can hold back the love of God which will follow us down even the darkest alleyways of our own making.

Today, this time in the desert is also one of those experiences I look back on and cling to as an affirmation of God's goodness and constant redemptive purpose in my life.

Moments like these are for me touchstone experiences. They are ones that I come back to in moments of doubt, worry, and fear.

If I was to draw a timeline of my life, they would be symbolised by pictures of cairns; those little piles of rocks, the altars that pilgrims

build to mark a significant place on their journey.

I have them written down in my journals too lest I forget because I am no different to the Israelites. Despite the repeated demonstrations of God's faithfulness, love, and mercy, I am nevertheless quite capable of grumbling whilst the sand from my place of rescue is still caught between my toes.

REFLECTION: PLACING THE CAIRNS IN YOUR LIFE JOURNEY

I would invite you to draw a representation of your life journey as you reflect on the scripture below:

Psalm 105: 1–5

Give praise to the Lord, proclaim his name;
　make known among the nations what he has done.
Sing to him, sing praise to him;
　tell of all his wonderful acts.
Glory in his holy name;
　let the hearts of those who seek the Lord rejoice.
Look to the Lord and his strength;
　seek his face always.
Remember the wonders he has done,
　his miracles, and the judgments he pronounced. . .

This is an exercise best not rushed which may benefit from being done over a number of days. You can do this in any way that appeals to you. Options might include:

📖 a timeline on which you highlight the events that have shaped it

📖 a symbolic representation of your journey:

- using a landscape with its mountain top highs, its valley lows, its rough seas, its quiet waters, its flowing rivers, its swamplands, its well-tended pastures, its dense undergrowth, its dark woodlands, its sheltered glades, its rocky obstacles, and its straight or winding paths

- using a tree with its roots, its rough and smooth bark, its strong trunk, its gnarled burls, its lichens and nests, its bifurcating branches, its leaves, and its fruit

- using the imagery of the seasons: spring moments of new beginnings, the colourful and abundant times of summer, those periods, sometimes painful, of autumnal letting go or of fruition in the bounty of harvest and the times of withdrawal, stillness and waiting of winter

Invite the Holy Spirit to guide you as you do this. Ask Him also to help you place the cairns which mark those touchstone experiences when special grace was poured out to you in some way.

✠

Allow the Holy Spirit to lead your response in prayer as you finish.

✠

Reviewing my life as a whole, and noticing the many markers of God's saving presence as I did so, was an exercise of the retreat but one I have come back to since as I have had reason to place more cairns along the way. However, the retreat didn't just encourage me to look back and notice the big moments, it asked me to be more attentive to the present moment; gathering up and noticing the many ways God graces the ordinary as well as the extraordinary. Sometimes we capture these moments as they are happening, other times it is as we review the day finished that we see the blessings.

This **discipline of reviewing our days** is one of the best ways I know of laying down a firm foundation in Christ.[†] The more we notice God's goodness to us, the more we will trust God and act on that trust in His continuing and daily renewed grace. God is good.

The retreat is long behind me but this process of review has remained with me. Although there have been times when I have only done it periodically, that is no longer the case. Today I have a discipline, practised almost daily with a friend, of sharing by text or email the blessings from the previous day(s). We try to be specific about what these were rather than general. We have been doing this for several years now and it encourages us both as we see God active in each other's lives. Further, it gives us fuel for the lean days when worry and doubt might or do take hold.

---

†See Appendix 2, Contemplating our Daily Lives.

REFLECTION:

CAPTURING AND SHARING DAILY BLESSINGS WITH A FRIEND

If this is the sort of discipline you would find helpful, and especially if you are currently seeking the grace of trust, then I would encourage you to do this with a willing friend. You don't have to do it on an open-ended basis. You could do it for a month, see what you uncover and decide between you the merit of continuing.

✠

Everything I learnt during my time of retreat was beneficial. All the exercises were positive in intent and aimed at helping me to deepen my relationship with God. However, that does not mean that the Spiritual Exercises are without grit, avoiding those dark places which undermine our relationship with God – not at all.

We all know what it is like to find ourselves in a mess of our own making, to find our joy stolen from us or, as Paul might say, repeatedly to find that we do that which we do not wish to do but we have done it anyway.[†] God invites us to root our lives in the pure waters of His love and yet there can be times when we find we are up to our ankles in a murky sludge. This despite God's saving action which, whilst ultimately covering our mistakes and drawing us into the relationship with Him that can transform us, does not automatically keep us from our errant ways.

[†] See Romans 7:14–21 and, in particular, verse 19.

We all carry fractures and breaks. These are the effects of living in a fallen world; damage which can mean we struggle to choose God's love. We opt instead for paths that lead us somewhere other than the Spirit would choose for us to go.

The Spiritual Exercises explore in some depth the sinfulness of the world and the role of sin in our own lives. The surprise for me as I went through this process was that, whilst I was indeed sinful and wilful, and whilst the wages of sin are death, so **much of my sinfulness was the effect of brokenness** and God's judgement revealed above all his love and mercy.

In my particular case, I discovered, fear is a significant driver in my life. Not the fear of any kind of physical harm but the fear of failure. It is not that I simply want to be successful, I want to please others by being successful because that is how I think I will be most loveable.

This is twisted, of course, but I don't think I am unusual in having, in effect, a tape in my head that says, 'I am most loveable if...' For someone else that sentence might be completed as follows: 'if I am the life of the party' or 'if I am helpful' or 'if I am no bother' or 'if I am clever' or 'if I am funny', and so on.

There is nothing intrinsically wrong with wishing to be successful but it created a general fear of failure and a specific need to manage that fear as I could not always guarantee to be the best. I addressed this need by trying to be in control as much as possible. I felt safest if I knew what to expect and could manage how to navigate a situation. I wanted to choose at what level to engage with something so that, if all went to plan, I could be successful and please at that level.

I felt less vulnerable when I was in control but this then meant that I chose to sit on the throne of my own life. If I was on the throne then God was not and so this sin was, in effect, idolatry. It is not that I worshipped myself but I placed myself where God should have been. I would make the decisions even as I acknowledged God as Lord. This contradictory stance was not so much the result of conscious disobedience as a lack of understanding and awareness of how fear manipulated me.

Much became clear as I began to perceive who I was in all my humanity and, therefore, my frailty. My deeper motivations were also revealed. I wanted to please God in the ways I served Him but on my terms; in ways I felt safest. My criteria for feeling safe did not include Sabbath with its still waters and green pastures and so I had successfully filled my days to the brim. My attachment to safety also required me to impress and court the good opinion of others despite the inevitable consequence and inherent paradox that I was then vulnerable to those opinions.

Uncovering our brokenness and sinfulness gives us self-knowledge which can be very helpful for steering us round certain temptations. However, it is not for the purpose of self-empowerment. Rather it is to give us the wisdom to realise that we can neither overcome our sinfulness in our own strength nor can we heal ourselves. We need God on both counts.

Further, the deepening experience of God's mercy embeds another fundamental script in our hearts; that He loves me as I am and He loves you as you are. There is nothing you or I can add or take away that will change that.

When I make decisions led by fear or a desire to control which, of course, I still at times do, I nearly always find that these are not life-giving. It is as though I have placed myself in a tomb. However,

I have not deliberately chosen such confinement. I want to choose life and so today, when I wake up to the fact that I am in this familiar but suffocating space, I listen for the voice of Jesus much as Lazarus must have heard it, saying, 'Sarah, come out!'[†]

I have found my way back to the tomb often enough over the years to have discovered that, even if there is colossal personal disappointment in finding yet again I have chosen that which ultimately harms me, nonetheless when I come forth once more into the light in response to the invitation of Jesus to 'Come out', the resurrection is somehow greater each time. I am a little freer, a little less bound, a little less attached to whatever had led me back to that tomb in the first place. God is good.

REFLECTION: COME OUT!

The story of Lazarus being raised from the dead is a helpful one to contemplate when considering what in our lives might wrap us in grave clothes and entomb us. The story is told in John 11:1–44. However, whilst I would invite you to read the whole passage for context and so that you can enter into this scene more easily, I would suggest contemplating in greater depth verses 38–44.

If you do identify with Lazarus, hear Jesus say your name as He stands in the open, free, and light-filled space outside the tomb inviting you to come out.

✠

[†] See the story of Lazarus in John 11.

There are those present who are asked afterwards to help Lazarus free of his grave clothes. Who in your life might help you if you need it?

✠

A reminder of the suggested steps:-

Centre, Read, Contemplate, Review, Journal

Another lesson from my desert days which has remained with me is about the nature of sacrifice. When I was very busy in the mid-nineties, I used to rationalise and accept my fatigue as being a consequence of wanting to live my life as a daily offering to God; giving my time, if need be, sacrificially. Sacrifice, I reasoned, was part and parcel of the Christian way and so what was a little fatigue in the scheme of things. It was a small cross to bear really.

The Christian walk is cross-shaped; that is true. There is indeed a denying of the self, a taking up of the cross, and a willingness to follow Jesus involved.[†] However, with that in mind, as I followed Jesus through the many gospel stories, I could not help noticing that Jesus does not do everything every time that He could. For example, whilst He physically healed many people, He did not necessarily heal everyone who might have needed physical healing. He often withdrew to be with His Father avoiding the crowds that would pursue Him.[*]

---

†See Mark 8:34–37.

*See, for example, Matthew 5:1 or Matthew 8:18.

Jesus sacrificed heaven to be amongst us and then He sacrificed His life to save us. Therefore, what does the example of His life tell us about sacrifice? We cannot know what interaction might have occurred within the God-head before Jesus broke into our world at Christmas. However, we do know what happened prior to the cross.

In Gethsemane, Jesus sought His Father regarding this approaching sacrifice in prayer. Looking to God, especially when significant sacrifice is involved, is the wisdom that recognises that it is only if God is at the heart of that sacrifice and equipping us that we will be able to sustain it. Seeking His guidance and confirmation that this is what He is truly asking of us is crucial. For if God is not asking sacrifice of us then instead of faith, hope, and love, there is likely eventually to be resentment, anger, and disappointment. Encouraging sacrifice without appropriate discernment is one of the devil's ways to dress up like an angel and mislead us.[†]

In this context, it is worth remembering the forty days that Jesus spent in the desert as He began His ministry. This was a time of testing but also a time when He was fortified and prepared for what lay ahead. When we reflect on the temptations the devil endeavours to snare Him with, these are all ones that look like saving action but are not the Father's purpose through the cross. Jesus heads into His three years of ministry with the clarity of knowing His Father's will and yet He still seeks his Father in prayer in Gethsemane when it comes to the final sacrifice of the cross.

[†]See Appendix 7, Frequently Asked Questions, regarding discernment.

Mark 14: 35–36

Going a little farther, he fell to the ground and prayed that if possible the hour might pass from him. "Abba, Father," he said, "everything is possible for you. Take this cup from me. Yet not what I will, but what you will."

Another clue about sacrifice is in the cross itself. The cross is not about death. It is about life. As a matter of discernment, a God-blessed sacrifice will always lead to life even if there is some dying in the process. If there is no life-giving fruit, have another long hard look at it and listen for God's guidance again.

Contemplation, solitude, learning to recognise God's voice, discovering my touchstone experiences, uncovering the manna that is poured so abundantly into my lap each day, learning my absolute need of God given the evidence of my frailty, and the recognition that I constantly need to discern God's voice to be able to follow Him, were all gifts of my desert journey. It was a time which laid the foundations in me of a stronger and more resilient faith.

At the end of the retreat, I sat down and wrote what I think of as a psalm about my desert experience. I offer it to you here as testimony to that time. God is good. He heard and answered the desire of my heart.

I was searching for that true experience;
the knowing you cannot deny or have taken from you.
I was looking for the strength for the miles yet to be walked
and the trials yet to be endured.
I desired to drink long and deeply from the very well of life itself;
to put down a root so deep I would never be thirsty.

I wanted to fulfil my purpose to love with all that I am
the One who loves me just as I am.

Jesus beckoned, hand outstretched,
"Come", He said to me,
"I will speak to your heart and you will know me."

I walked with my shoes.

I entered the desert realm;
holy ground.
Yet Jesus himself stooped and untied my shoes,
an act of infinite kindness and mercy,
not the severe judgement I deserved.

My shoes.
Symbols of my link to this earth;
creature of a fallen world and a perfect God.
Jesus exposed my feet and so
my vulnerability,
my insecurity;
the overwhelming fear that is always ready to annihilate me.

Jesus took me to the hilltops and said,
"Behold your throne."
And then, like a whisper carried faintly on a gentle breeze,
He said,
"Come, I will speak to your heart and you will know me."

But I see who I am and the knowledge is terrible.
Wait.
Knowledge is power.
I can carry on. . .

We travel together through the desert realm.
Is this my heart that is burning
as He invites me to look, to listen, and to understand?

"You know me as God. You must know me as man.
See my struggles.
See my temptations.
Know them as real.
Witness my love for my people.
Witness my fatigue, my frustration, my irritation.
Take note of the loneliness of the journey,
the pain of being misunderstood,
and the magnitude of the calling.
Experience my fear and my faith."

We walked together through the Holy Land.
We walked to Jerusalem.

"Don't go", say the tempters.
"Be King", say the deceivers.
"Hosanna to the Son of David", shout the admirers.

"Come Jesus", says His Father,
"Come, I will speak to your heart. Come, and do my work."

We walk to the garden in sorrow and dread.
We are pursued by the shadow of betrayal and fear.
We are upheld in the hope of life in abundance and life eternal.
Silence.
Let not the lamb speak or defend himself.

Death.
The road to life embraces death.
Paradox.

The sacrificial lamb lies before me and speaks,
"I sacrificed my life for you that you might live and not die.
I sacrificed for the love of life not for the love of death.
The road to life embraces death, it does not end there."

Consolation is not in the dying.
Consolation is in the life within the death and the life beyond it.

Consolation is in the obedience to the voice
that beckons you towards the light.
That invites you constantly
to take note that Jesus walked free from the tomb.

Will I let Him set me free?

I see my throne.
The seat wears the grooves of bearing my weight for years past.
It calls to me too in its familiarity.
Safe.

But the clouds of darkness are upon it
and the voice upon the wind is not gentle but vicious.
The hiss of fear.
There is no safety here.

I see my Saviour's throne.
Light blazes around it but it is empty.
Where is Jesus? O where is Jesus?
"I am here", says a voice.
"I am speaking to your heart.
I know who you are too.
But Sarah, knowledge is not power, it is hope"
"Allow me to love you.
Let me set you free each day.
Walk with me and both our hearts' desires will be fulfilled."

Amen.
My heart gives thanks.

Chapter 6

'Stonemover'

I emerged from the desert not long before our home landscape was about to change again. James was being posted for a second time to Australia. We would arrive in Melbourne just as all four digits of the year 1999 had clicked over into the year 2000. Not just a new year but a new millennium! Could there be a better moment to step out and do things differently without repeating old patterns of behaviour than the opportunity offered by yet another new beginning? I could take everything I had learnt in the desert and, in theory, begin to apply it.

I could continue to remain alert for the revelation of God's goodness and presence in my days whilst especially making sure that, as I took up new commitments, I did not just leap into any and everything as I had done previously. To that end, the retreat had suggested that an understanding of my vocation would help me with the process of discerning where to place my energies as God intended.

The word *vocation* is, on the surface, a simple one to understand. It comes from the Latin word *'vocatio'* which means a calling or a summons. If that calling is from God then it makes sense that, if I heed it, I will be where I am meant to be. My calling will be like identifying north with a compass; a point by which to navigate and discern next steps that are consistent with it. However, vocation is not a word we typically apply to everyone and certainly not a word I had ever applied to myself.

We usually speak of someone having a vocation when we recognise a true harmony between who they fundamentally are and what they do. For example, to the teacher who has a vocation to teach, teaching is not just a profession, it is an outward manifestation of an inner truth about who they were born and predisposed to be. They cannot help but teach whether in the classroom or out. Not all teachers have a vocation to teach but, for those who do, the calling they are responding to is to be true to themselves.

The example of a teacher comes to mind, rather than one of the other professions to which we sometimes ascribe the word vocation, because my husband James is one. His vocation is to teach. However, he only took up teaching as a profession in 2007 after twenty years in the oil industry where he had commercial and operational roles. Nevertheless, over all those years, he was still a teacher as he often found himself with side roles at work that involved teaching. He also led and taught bible studies and youth groups through church, and he expressed that part of himself at home not only with our boys but also with those of our friends willing to be introduced to bridge and the strategic board games that he so enjoys. James' vocation as a teacher may now be obvious in what he does but it was actually there all along, manifesting itself even when he did not have the job title to match.

However, most of us would probably not be aware of a predisposition towards one role or area of service over another.

There is not that obvious fit between who we are with our individual gifts, personality, and experience and what we do. We would simply not say that we had a vocation in that way. We might recognise that a vocational call to the ordained ministry or the mission field could come to any one of us from God. However, we would probably not apply the language of vocation to the broader call God makes to each one of us to serve.

This is because our common usage of the word places it apart to describe the few rather than the many. However, in the context of our faith in God, we do all have a vocation. I can be sure of that for He has uniquely created and fashioned each one of us and set us apart accordingly. Our *vocation* is God's call to us to be and to reveal the fullness of who we truly are in Him through all that we do. We are to give expression to the natural gifts we were born with and those spiritual gifts we received from His Holy Spirit, when we came to faith, in the unique context of our lives.

Jeremiah comes to mind at this point:

Jeremiah 1: 4 & 5
The word of the Lord came to me, saying,
"Before I formed you in the womb I knew you,
before you were born I set you apart;
I appointed you as a prophet to the nations."

Jeremiah's calling was to be a prophet to the nations. He was set apart to do so in a way that only he, Jeremiah, could.

In the New Testament, the apostle Peter offers another example of vocation:

John 1:42b

Jesus looked at him and said, "You are Simon son of John. You will be called Cephas" (which, when translated, is Peter).

Jesus gave him the name which declared his vocation for Cephas and Peter both mean 'rock'; the one in Aramaic, the other in Greek. Jesus also clarifies why he is the rock:

Matthew 16:18a

And I tell you that you are Peter, and on this rock I will build my church . . .

We could re-write that as follows:

Before I formed you in the womb, Simon, I knew you,

Before you were born I set you apart;

I appointed you as Peter, the rock on which I will build my church.

Simon was revealed to be Peter, with all that entailed, when he was fully who God created him to be through the transformative presence and work of the Holy Spirit in him.

God has a word for us in the same way that He had one for Jeremiah and Peter. He says:

"Before I formed you in the womb I knew you,

Before you were born I set you apart;

I appointed you as . . ."

God has filled in the blank but we have to discern how. As already noted, it will make sense of who we truly are given our gifts, both natural and spiritual, our personality, and life story.

Discovering our vocation, with its emphasis on understanding who we truly are in God, could suggest that the motivating purpose is self-fulfilment but, although that would follow, it is not, it is obedience. Living out our vocation is a way of keeping in step more easily with the Holy Spirit.[†] It is a way of putting God's Word into practice in our lives. We know from the story Jesus tells about the wise man that when we do that we are building our house on rock.[*]

Therefore, there are many benefits to our obedience; to answering the call to be truly ourselves as we surrender to the transformative impact and power of the Holy Spirit's presence in our lives. We lay down a strong and firm foundation in Him. We do not experience the inner dissonance of trying to be what we are not but rather the wellbeing of who we are. We produce and are blessed by the fruit that flows from living and keeping in step with the Holy Spirit: love, joy, peace, patience, kindness, goodness, faithfulness, gentleness and self-control.[‡] We can have confidence that, as a Good Shepherd, Jesus will lead us by still waters and green pastures; that He will ensure there is rest and the ease of yoke and burden He promises us.[§]

However, living out our vocation does not guarantee that the road we travel will be easy. As the Christ, Jesus is the Saviour but His vocation took Him on the hard road to the cross. Jeremiah

---

[†]Galatians 5:25
[*]Luke 6: 46–49
[‡]Galatians 5:22
[§]See Psalm 23:2 and Matthew 11:28–30.

became known as the weeping prophet, such was his grief and empathy for the fate of Judah.[†] Peter was indeed a founding father of the church but one who was crucified for his faith. The journey can be very bumpy but, if we are responding to His call, we can be confident that the Holy Spirit will equip, sustain, refresh, and provide for us in the right measure to enable us to meet the challenges as required. Our circumstances will not have the power to rob us of the Holy Spirit's gifts of peace and joy for we will be like the branches which, remaining in the vine, continue to produce fruit and experience the blessing of that relationship.[*]

God does not forsake us when we travel on a road of our own choosing but we have probably chosen our own strength and resources over His in so doing. It will be a harder road by consequence than it need be. This was my experience prior to the retreat as I gradually ran myself into the ground. However, even on that other path, God is ever with us calling us in His mercy and goodness to another way, His way; a way which reveals our vocation.

When we live into the fullness of who God has created us to be and who He is further shaping us to be by the presence of His Holy Spirit within us, we will serve His kingdom and be His light and presence in the wider world as He intended.

The apostle Paul uses the analogy of the body to explain how we all have an essential role to play to ensure the health and wellbeing of the church which is Christ's body.[‡] We need

---

[†]See Jeremiah 9:1 among other examples.

[*]See John 16:33 and John 15: 1–11.

[‡]See 1 Corinthians 12:12–27.

to understand who we are within that body. For to play the wrong part, too many parts, or no part is to harm the whole, and to hold back its ability to be a witness to God as intended within this world. I think back to the example of the spoon in chapter two when I wrote that, in 1997, I was probably busy being a teaspoon, a dessert spoon, and a ladle. I am reminded that this was not only wrong for me but also meant others were not getting the opportunity to fulfil the part that God intended for them.

Remaining true to our vocation does not mean that we are excused from ever doing something in passing that is helpful and good because it does not sit within the scope of our vocation. Vocation may clarify and direct us to our main area of service and ministry but we are always called to be a good neighbour.

REFLECTION: HOW AM I SERVING?

Take some time in prayer to contemplate how you are currently serving God in your church and wider community.

✠

📖 What led you to undertake these commitments?
📖 Whose call were you answering?

✠

If you have already done this in some measure in response to the invitation on page 39, you might like to refer back to any journal notes that you took at the time and hold these again in prayer.

····➔

In either case, don't seek to judge what you are doing; just notice what led you to where you are now. Hold any revelation that may arise before God and seek His further guidance and discernment as to next steps.

✠

Arriving in Australia, I knew that to take the right next steps I needed to understand my vocation. However, although I could believe I had a vocation, I had not finished the retreat with any clarity as to what it was. I had prayed and discussed the issue at length with my Spiritual Director and, whilst I had some helpful insights, I had no more than that.

It is time to assert again that God is good. The move was all the more timely as it meant I neatly escaped the considerable dilemma of what to pick up or not from my previous commitments. It also offered me a further period of grace, as no one would be expecting me to get stuck in quickly following such a major relocation. I had time to keep praying over this point of vocation.

However, struggle as I did to hear God's word for me, discernment of my vocation came no easier in Australia than it had in Scotland. In the absence of clarity, I had been encouraged to pay close attention to what others said about me. As a result, I noticed two words standing out: they were that I was 'articulate' and 'passionate'. This had led my Spiritual Director in Scotland to suggest that perhaps my vocation was one of advocacy or even prophecy!

I did my best to try and bring an open mind to the suggestion that I could be an Advocate or a Prophet and, doing so, I understood why they could present as options. However, despite their far-reaching applications, they left me feeling, paradoxically, constricted. It was like trying to wear a shoe that is too small; I was not unwilling, I just could not seem to make either one comfortable. This feeling of mismatch might have been evidence enough for the discernment that they therefore did not fit but I had another reason for hesitating as well.

I knew that, however passionate I could be, however much driving energy I could have, I wasn't always revved up to that intensity. I could identify moments that had felt blessed with God's presence which had a much quieter and gentler dynamic in play, moments when I had said very little, if anything, at all.

I continued to pray and wait.

Eventually the breakthrough came as I asked this question: 'Lord, who do you say I am?'[†]

As I sat with a deep desire to hear His reply, I was reminded of the familiar story of Lazarus being raised from the dead and was prompted to read John 11 again. I was struck by this verse:

John 11:39a

"Take away the stone," he said.

I had never before noticed that there was a 'Stonemover' but I had an immediate sense of identification with this individual whoever they were. I thought to myself, 'that is it', I move stones. It was completely clear to me. Stones come in all sizes. There are great big ones that require huge energy to shift and there are little tiny ones that are bounced out the way by little more than one's passing

---

[†]This echoes Christ's question to Peter in Matthew 16:13–20 and specifically verse 15. Also see Mark 8:27–30 and Luke 9:18–20.

presence or a well-timed nudge. This seemed to capture what I perceived as my range – sometimes passionate, sometimes quiet but, whichever it was, and whether by words or my presence, looking to do something that opened up a way or created the potential for understanding, change, or progress.

REFLECTION ON VOCATION: WHO DO YOU SAY I AM?

'Who do you say I am?' is a question you can ask too if you do not have clarity about your vocation.

You may hear God's reply immediately when you ask this question or you may need to ask and wait patiently for the reply to be revealed over a period of time.

It may help to pray over your gifts. What are they? What are the gifts you were born with and what are the spiritual gifts you have been further blessed with? What sort of personality are you? What have been some of your formative experiences to date and what do they reveal?

A helpful scripture to contemplate as you do this would be Jesus' call of Nathanael in John 1:43–51 focusing on verses 47–48.

✠

Centre, Read, Contemplate, Review, Journal

Asking your friends or being attentive to what they say about you can be helpful too.

Ask God to lead you in your reflections. Let Him show you how He sees you. Let Him call you.

Although I was fairly confident my vocation was as a Stonemover, as I sat with that revelation in the weeks thereafter, I also discerned confirmation in the realisation that being a Stonemover was not only consistent with my strengths but also with my weaknesses. Although this may sound surprising, it is not. When we are living into who God has intended us to be, we are walking closely with Him. The devil's best tactic in those circumstances is not to tempt us with something obviously off key and out of kilter which we would spot but to tempt us with something that is only a slight twist away from what it should be.

One of the biggest risks for me when I am supporting friends or dealing with a situation is the temptation to go from my assigned and limited role of moving the stone to the next step of saving who or whatever is happening. Saving, though, is Christ's unique role. In the context of the story of Lazarus, there are lots of different characters fulfilling a range of roles but it was Jesus alone who could call Lazarus to life.

It is easy to see how I might confuse moving a stone with the next step of Christ calling someone to life but, when I do make that mistake, the consequences are neither good for me nor the focus of my endeavours. I usually end up overwhelmed and unable to sustain what was never asked or expected of me in the first place. My greatest strength and my greatest weakness are just a step apart which is probably why it is so easy to move from obedience to sin not just for me but for all of us.

Understanding at last my vocation, all I needed was a flyer which said, 'Stonemovers required'. However, I have yet to find a church ministry or profession which advertises for my particular skills in that way. I imagine that for many of us our vocation will not sit neatly and obviously aligned with a profession like teacher or doctor, or a ministry like preaching might. I could be a Stonemover in countless situations and within the context of any number of professions. I remained and remain dependent on God to reveal and point the way as the path does not come with billboard signage and because old habits are hard to break as I discovered quite quickly.

REFLECTION ON OUR TEMPTATIONS

The temptations of Jesus in the desert are very helpful for understanding how the devil operates and can lead us astray.

I would invite you to contemplate this story in either Matthew 4: 1–11 or Luke 4:1–13 and to do so twice. The first time do so from the perspective of Jesus paying attention to how the temptations He faces are peculiarly well targeted given His vocation as the Son of God to save the world.

✠

The second time through, especially if you have a sense of your own vocation, place yourself within the story and invite God to reveal to you how the devil tempts you and the replies that you can give to fend him off.

✠

Centre, Read, Contemplate, Review, Journal

After exactly a year in Melbourne, we moved to Perth, Western Australia in January 2001. I arrived knowing I was a Stonemover and ready to serve. Indeed, so ready, I leapt straight in as though the retreat and subsequent period of waiting on God in Melbourne had never happened. I can be taught but I am slow to learn! Our new church had a recently appointed minister who needed an administrator. I could help and I offered to do so with barely a thought, let alone a prayer, on a part-time and voluntary basis. It was a mistake.

It was a role that did have stonemoving aspects to it for it involved setting up new systems and shifting things to do so. However, it was also a role that played to my weaknesses as there was a lot of change involved for the church which was challenging. My temptation was to save everyone affected by those changes from the disturbance they caused.

When I took the time to contemplate my daily life during this period, I could see that I carried the role increasingly as a heavy yoke and a burden; I struggled to find God's presence with me in it, not because He had abandoned me but because He had not called me into the role in the first place. It was not my vocation. Ever faithful, He was alongside me nonetheless but calling and drawing me towards something quite different; to move stones through contemplation.

By 2002, I had been practising contemplative prayer for five years and knew that it blessed me greatly even if I sometimes failed to apply well what I learnt from it. However, I knew very few people who also used contemplative prayer as part of their discipleship walk. I began to wonder whether I could share the blessings of this type of prayer with others. Tentatively, I held a meeting. The response from those who attended was very positive, which was encouraging. I also, significantly, discerned a response of joy within myself. Further meetings followed.

On returning to Scotland at the start of 2003, there was a time of waiting on God as I wanted to discern how He would lead me to be a Stonemover now that I was back in the familiar pasture of our former church. As I waited, I shared with various church friends about the contemplative prayer group I had started in Australia and there were two who were particularly keen to come along to such a group if I started one. Remembering the joy I had felt in Australia as I introduced others to contemplative prayer, and on the basis that where two or three are gathered in His name, Christ is also, I felt a ministry in contemplative prayer was my way forward.[†]

However, it turned out that there was enough interest within the congregation to start two groups; a daytime and an evening one. The groups met monthly for an hour covering the same material developed around a theme.[*] Early on, a pattern for the meetings emerged: after a time of centring, I would lead two further contemplative exercises.

The first looked to open up the theme in a universal way and the second looked to take the insights from that to a personal level. To keep it fresh and engaging, I would vary the centring prayers and methods of contemplation I used. We might pray reflectively over an appropriate object, photograph, or a DVD clip, or we might pray contemplatively or meditatively with Scripture. We might do a prayer walk, or sit in simple silence before God or we might reflect

---

[†]Matthew 18:20

[*]To give you an idea of the themes, just a few examples would be: "Contentment", "Perspective", "The Foolishness of the Cross", "The heart of Christ", "God the Rock", "Stepping out in Faith", "Compassion", "Boldness", "God who is rich in Mercy", "Beloved", "Thanksgiving", and "Abundant Grace".

over his presence in our daily lives. An example of a contemplative prayer session is offered in Appendix 5.

Whatever the approach used, the idea was not to 'do' a theme in an hour but, like a stone dropping into a pool, the expectation was that its impact would ripple on afterwards expanding that initial experience.

There were also opportunities to share insights between the exercises but no compulsion to do so. The emphasis for those attending remained always first and foremost on gathering to listen for God's personal word and revelation for them. A word which they could share and offer their fellow pilgrims but could never assume was what someone else needed to hear at that time even though others might be encouraged or challenged by it.

Meeting in a group to do this gave those who were drawn by the idea of contemplative prayer, but uncertain about how to begin, an opportunity when they could gather with others and be guided through the process. They gained experience and familiarity with it which then built their confidence to do it alone.

It was stonemoving because what I did was to 'open up' an opportunity for Jesus to be heard as He called those who attended the meetings – and other events I went on to organise – to a deeper experience of life in Him. The ideas and themes came to me like gifts. I would live with the theme for at least the month before we did it and sometimes longer, allowing it to develop and take shape as I felt God leading me with it. I felt responsible for leading the meetings but I did not feel responsible for how God would work through the meetings. The outcomes were not mine to control; I knew I could trust God with those.

I soon discovered just how dynamic God's Word and work in

us is as, through what was shared, I could see the same material touching and blessing people in entirely personal and different ways. I understood and could see that this was God's work in and through me; the temptation to go further than was asked of me was held in check.

Being a Stonemover is a whole life experience though; it is who I am, and I carry that in to all my relationships and activities. If I mostly manage to spot and resist the temptation to do more than move stones within the context of this ministry, I am not always as alert the rest of the time. Although aware of the risk, I can still get it wrong. The transforming work of Christ in me is a lifelong process – of course.

I started the contemplative prayer ministry at my church in 2003 and, although I still often take the lead role, gradually it has evolved to include other leaders which not only brings other voices and approaches but also contributes to its sustainability and fruitfulness as a ministry.

Over the years, regardless of the backdrop of my circumstances, contemplative prayer has helped me to experience the extraordinary and abundant grace of God. As I have led others to deepen their journeys using this tool of contemplative prayer, I have felt myself coming alive in new and deeper ways as well. I have experienced joy, peace, hope, love, and many other blessings in and through the exercise of this ministry because, I believe, I have been where God was calling me to be, doing what He was calling me to do; being who He has created me to be.

There is no describing the gratitude that awakens in my soul as I write that; gratitude on so many levels.

Gratitude, in a first instance, for all the personal blessings I have experienced. The preparation and prayer the meetings require constantly point out to me God's love and mercy, His might and power, and His absolute faithfulness. He has continued to answer my 1997 prayer for a deeper more intimate relationship with Him and helped head knowledge to find its way to my heart. Prior to the accident, I was never conscious of what this was cumulatively adding up to but the tap root had been drilling deep.

Gratitude for the privilege I have enjoyed of sharing in the walk of so many of my fellow pilgrims in this way. There has been real benefit in learning from and being inspired by their journeys.

Gratitude for the equipment this ministry has given me. When I am not coping, when I am adrift, when I am at odds with my life or when I don't have a sense of God's presence, I do know that contemplation is a helpful tool. It is not the only one to be sure, but I find it especially helpful for finding my way back to the One who calls me beloved and at whose feet I can lay my fears and troubles.

My deepest gratitude though is for the heart-felt knowledge and awareness it has given me of God's all-surpassing goodness as my constant Saviour, Guide and Companion. It has taught me to expect to find God in my days and it has reminded, encouraged, and invited me to be correspondingly attentive for Him; **to be awake**.

Chapter 7

The Heron's Portion

I lean my head against the train window and look intently at the bank of the river we are passing. Will I be blessed with a sighting today or not? I am looking out for a heron. Sometimes I see one at this point in my journey, sometimes not.

When I do, what I notice is its patience; it is so still, so full of focus and confidence as it waits on its next meal. It would not wait in this spot if it knew its waiting would be fruitless. It is alert in anticipation. It reminds me of Psalm 27:

> ### *Psalm 27:13–14*
> *I remain confident of this:*
> *I will see the goodness of the Lord*
> *in the land of the living.*
> *Wait for the Lord;*
> *be strong and take heart and wait for the Lord.*

The heron speaks to me as I travel south to see Sam who is now in Glasgow at Scotland's specialist spinal injuries unit.

On Sam's first day in the unit, his consultant had made certain things very clear to James and me:

📖 Sam was now tetraplegic – affected by paralysis in all four limbs

📖 He would not walk again

📖 He would require the support of a full-time carer for the rest of his life

We were given this blunt news even though it was only a week since the accident and Sam's spinal cord was still in spinal shock. Therefore, affected by inflammation which causes maximum paralysis in the short term but, given an incomplete injury which was the case with Sam, leaves open the potential for improvements as the swelling subsides.[†]

I had no words for the ache that I felt. I would have prayed but I could not articulate my pain such was its force. I felt utterly devastated by the darkness of the doctor's words and what they meant for Sam. This would be no passing difficulty; his life was radically altered by this injury.

Into the void, words for the enormity of what was happening were given to me by the psalms.

Psalm 46:1–3

God is our refuge and strength,
  an ever-present help in trouble.
Therefore we will not fear,
  though the earth give way
    and the mountains fall into the heart of the sea,
though its waters roar and foam
  and the mountains quake with their surging.

[†]An injury is only called *complete* if the spinal cord has been fully severed. If there has been damage to the cord but parts of it remain connected, it is an *incomplete* injury and recovery, reflecting where the spinal cord is still functioning, will gradually manifest.

Psalm 34:18

The Lord is close to the broken-hearted
and saves those who are crushed in spirit.

There was, indeed, giving way and falling, roaring and foaming, quaking, surging, and crushing. It was every bit of that. The psalmist gave my pain expression but also pointed to the place of refuge, strength, hope, salvation, and recovery – God.

There would be no way through this other than the hard way. However, if I could wait in trust, holding on to the invitation to stay awake, God would provide for me. Just as the heron waits for the fish, I would also wait for God. He would sustain and equip me. He would show me 'the goodness of the Lord in the land of the living' as He transformed this ill for good.[†] So I would look for the heron as the train passed the river and remember to be alert.

The opportunities to see the heron were frequent, if not guaranteed. The unit is a six hour round trip from our home near Aberdeen. James and I worked out a routine to ensure that between us, over the 7 months Sam was in the unit, we visited him every day but also came home to support Andrew and each other. We would travel together at weekends by car and during the week we would travel by train.

To limit consecutive days of travel, I would do the return journey on Mondays and Wednesdays whilst James did it on Tuesdays. On Thursdays I would travel down and stay overnight returning on the Friday. One of the early practical signs of God's provision was numerous offers of a bed in Glasgow. These included one

---

[†]Psalm 27:13

from the sister of one of our good friends in Australia which I accepted. In fact, Libby provided more than a bed, as a retired doctor, she understood the complexity of Sam's recovery. She gave me an opportunity to talk about the evolving situation, which I appreciated, without the need of detailed explanations which usually required emotional energy from me.

Although tiring, the commute became part of God's provision too. I did not use the time in a planned manner. I used the time mostly just to be. I would sit and allow the train to carry me – **God to carry me**. I had for years done centring prayers which encouraged me to release the weight of holding myself to God thus reflecting in my posture the trust expressed in prayer that it is God who truly holds us in being. As I look back now on these journeys, I can see that the train was a place of prayer whether there were words of prayer or not as I usually sat there leaning on God.

The journey to Glasgow by train is incredibly beautiful. Heading south, the train hugs the North Sea coastline until it swings westward along the river Tay from Dundee to Perth. It travels on through the hills to Gleneagles and Stirling as the peaks of the Trossachs become visible to the west. Eventually green countryside meets the urban edges of Glasgow and very quickly thereafter the journey is over. It was indeed a precious time full of unexpected gift and grace.

As I contemplated the North Sea, I found an image for the vastness of God's love. It comforted me. On wild and stormy days, the rolling breakers communicated messages of God's power and might; His strength to move obstacles and reshape the landscape. I received hope. On foggy days, when the view was cut off and there was only the immediacy of the train, I was reminded that He was not out there beyond my reach but, by His Holy Spirit, in me as close and constant as my next heartbeat and breath. When visible, the horizon could pull me forward to the future and away from the present; it could stir fear in me for all the unknowns. The fog countered with a call to the present where I AM awaited me and reassured me that He was in that moment where He would provide for me, if I would be in that moment too.

The river offered me not only the heron but also, with its greater stillness than the sea, reflections of the surrounding countryside. Sometimes not only every detail of the landscape was visible on the water's surface but, in moments of absolute calm, some of what lay in the water's depths was revealed in passing as well.

I found the still waters of the river extending an invitation to me to surrender my inner turbulence to God so that I might not only receive the gift of His peace but also reflect and reveal the presence, His presence, on which that peace depended. Trouble, Jesus says is unavoidable but being troubled is not.

REFLECTION: REVEALING THE DEPTHS

Turbulence on the surface of water masks depths which are revealed when water is in profound peace. If you have a river near where you live, I would encourage you to take a walk along it, if you can, contemplating how the water moves. Especially pay attention to the different moods of the river; eddies of calm compared with spots where the water might rush and surge. What do you see on the surface or in the depths? What is revealed?

✠

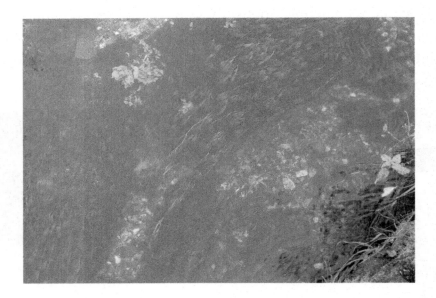

If you do not have a river nearby, you could simply fill the sink with water and place within its depths some stones or other items. Stir the water with your hands, create turbulence. Contemplate what you are doing and reflect on what you are seeing.

✠

John 16:33

I have told you these things, so that in me you may have peace. In this world you will have trouble. But take heart! I have overcome the world.

Jesus never asks us to deny the hard reality of our circumstances nor does He suggest short-cutting round them. Rather He urges us to trust that He has overcome the world through the power of the cross and, with our hearts rooted in that knowledge, to receive His promised gift of peace:

John 14:27

Peace I leave with you; my peace I give you. I do not give to you as the world gives. Do not let your hearts be troubled and do not be afraid.

Surrendering the tumult of my emotions to God was not easy and, therefore, I did not always respond to God's invitation to do so. However, whenever the river waters were particularly still, I would hear again the invitation to trust Him and, if I did, I would experience the grace of 'peace beyond all understanding'[†] carrying me along and bearing witness to the God-who-is-with-me.

The daily journeys to the spinal unit gave a structure to my days. However, the paving beneath my feet which enabled me to step through each day was laid down by the practical love and prayers of the many people who surrounded us. God is good.

Our families and friends were, of course, quick to provide support

---

[†]See Philippians 4:7

in whatever ways they could. My parents came and stayed with us for three months helping with the basic daily tasks of shopping, washing, cooking, and cleaning so I could focus my energies where they were most needed. Sam was sent thoughtful gifts to help with the hours of sheer tedium life in hospital entails along with countless cards of encouragement and hope. Over time many made the journey to visit him; often travelling up from England or further afield.

Within the mix of support, the church, the body of Christ, stands out, in particular. We felt the love of God given tangible expression as it reached out to hold us and to walk alongside us. A care that was not only faithfully and consistently offered over the months Sam was in the unit but continues to be shown for us now as well. Indeed over the months and years since the accident, we have had the privilege of witnessing our church as the bride of Christ; resplendent and beautiful, at its very best.

There are many practical examples of their support. In the immediate aftermath of the accident, our fridge and freezer were filled to overflowing with delicious meals and treats. James was helped with lifts to the hospital. One neighbour and friend regularly walked our dog for us, and not just for a week or two, but throughout all the months Sam was in the unit.

There were visits as people would stop by to say a brief hello with gifts, flowers or cards. One Monday morning, the doorbell went when I was at home sorting out Sam's clothes. The unit had advised me that to avoid pressure sores Sam would not be able to wear any clothing with pockets, buttons, studs, or heavy seams over the area of his bottom. Jeans, in particular, were not advisable as their fabric and design were harsh on the skin. Sam had many pairs of jeans and, as I removed them from his cupboard, I was in floods of tears at the thought that he no longer had that sartorial choice. The doorbell caught me in the midst of my misery.

I answered to find a friend from church standing there with the flowers that would have been in the church sanctuary the previous day; a gift from the church to say they were remembering us. The flowers were lovely and appreciated but it was her presence that was especially timely and helped. She could change nothing but she lovingly encouraged me to keep trusting God and by the time she left, although it still hurt, I felt strengthened.

Again many made the journey to visit Sam at the unit including our minister and the elders of our church, who went to pray over him in keeping with Scripture:

James 5:14

Is anyone among you sick? Let them call the elders of the church to pray over them and anoint them with oil in the name of the Lord.

We were also surrounded by their intercession. A week of 24/7 prayer was immediately organised as our church family got on its knees for us. Our evolving needs were shared and prayed over through the church prayer sheet during the months thereafter.

Other Christian friends engaged their churches – often our former churches from our times travelling and living abroad – in praying for us too. Friends of Sam's set up a 'Pray for Sam' Facebook page. Very quickly membership of this group expanded and, before long, it included members from across the world that we had never met but who, via this social network, became aware of our situation and expressed their support and concern in messages and prayer.

Mobile technology, especially useful as I was travelling so much, gave my friends the opportunity to send me scriptures and prayers by text message. These were invariably beautifully worded and full of such encouragement that I quickly realised that I could not bear to delete them, although I was going to have to, as my phone at the time had very limited storage capacity. I bought a journal and began to copy them into it instead. Over the time Sam was in hospital I filled three journals with over a 1000 text messages; each one precious, each one creating a solid pathway for me to walk on.

I responded to these friends by text with a weekly update on Friday mornings and with news as it happened; thanksgiving when I arrived to find there had been an improvement in Sam's condition, and requests for prayer when Sam's energy and physical resources were stretched to their limit.

There are some wonderful bible verses that are now written on my heart because they were either repeatedly sent to me or repeatedly experienced. The verse most often sent to us, to encourage confidence that God would yet redeem this tragedy, was:

Jeremiah 29:11

" . . . For I know the plans I have for you," declares the Lord, "plans to prosper you and not to harm you, plans to give you hope and a future."

The psalms and scriptures sent to me also gave words to prayers I could not voice. Often I was too tired to know how to marshal my thoughts tidily into coherent sentences of prayer. I would just hold Sam close to my heart and draw strength from passages like the one below which reminded me that I was led by a gentle and Good Shepherd who also carried Sam close to His heart.

Isaiah 40:11

He tends his flock like a shepherd:
He gathers the lambs in his arms
and carries them close to his heart;
he gently leads those that have young.

I trusted that the prayers of God's people, who surrounded us on every side, were putting into words what I could not. Psalm 125 gave me an image of what the church can be for us; it is like the mountains that surround Jerusalem, the embodied presence of God:

Psalm 125:1–2

Those who trust in the Lord are like Mount Zion,
which cannot be shaken but endures forever.
As the mountains surround Jerusalem,
so the Lord surrounds his people
both now and forevermore.

REFLECTION: THE WEATHER

Life can throw every type of challenge at us. Knowing scriptures that encourage us to remain rooted in God, seeking from Him the relevant help we need to face those circumstances, is a beneficial equipping for us all.

····→

We can discover and receive the resources we need in the heat of the moment, as I did, when people sent me messages with passages from Scripture to encourage me. God is good in this way. However, we can also prepare ourselves.

The weather provides us with helpful shorthand for thinking about our current circumstances and the equipment we might need for handling it. Sunny weather may only have us reaching for our sunglasses but, if it is scorching hot, we will need more water than usual too. In wet weather it may be that an umbrella is enough or, as the rain pours without cease and floods threaten, we may need sandbags.

Windy conditions may have us looking for cover and dark or misty ones looking for extra light. The circumstances dictate the need and being prepared, or knowing how to be prepared, can make all the difference to how we live through the challenge of what is happening.

What is the weather like in your life at the moment? Invite the Holy Spirit to guide your reflection as you consider which of the descriptions below best describes life for you just now.

Sunny
Cloudy with Sunny Intervals
Overcast with heavy Cloud
Light Showers
Heavy Showers
Thundery Showers

Hail Showers
Snow Showers
Fog
Mist
High Winds
Sand Storms

When you have discerned which weather description best relates to your current circumstances, you might like to pray now or later with the scriptures suggested below under the heading which is most appropriate to help with those weather conditions. You might also like to make a note of other scriptures which are already meaningful to you and fall under these sorts of headings as, of course, these are just a few of countless options.

Sunglasses:	Psalm 100; Psalm 92:1–5
Water Bottles	John 4:13 & 14; Jeremiah 17:7–8
Umbrellas	John 15:18–19; John 14: 1; Psalm 20
Windbreaks	Mark 4:35–41; Psalm 62:1–2: Ephesians 6:10–11
Hot Water Bottles	Romans 8:37–39; 1 John 3:1a
Lighthouses	Isaiah 60:19; Proverbs 3: 5 & 6; Ezekiel 34:11–12; Micah 6:8
Sand Bags	Isaiah 43:1–3a; Psalm 18:1–2 and 16–19

✠

Centre, Read, Contemplate, Review, Journal

I was alert and on the lookout for God's transforming goodness and I was not disappointed. Like the heron, I was being sustained by the revelations and blessings of the train journey, by Scripture, and by the constant feed of kindness from everyone we knew. I expect that for each individual who blessed us in some way, most would feel that their contribution was small and insignificant. It wasn't.

I prayed contemplatively more than once with the story of Jesus healing the paralysed man; each time I was looking for hope and solace in this especially pertinent story of miraculous healing.[†] When I imagined the paralysed man being lowered through the roof into the presence of Jesus, I pictured the church at one corner of the mat, our families at another corner, our friends at the third corner, and James, Andrew, and I at the fourth. This was a group effort, everyone was needed.

All those many small individual acts put together became something substantial. Like the Israelites receiving daily the manna they needed to survive in the wilderness as they fled Egypt, we all received enough of what we needed for the given day, Sam included.[*] I could find a solution for storing my text messages but I could not store my strength. It was renewed every morning in a way that recalls these words of Lamentations:

Lamentations 3:22–24
Because of the Lord's great love we are not consumed,
for his compassions never fail.

[†]See Matthew 9:1–8 or Mark 2:1–12 or Luke 5:17–26.
[*]See Exodus 16.

They are new every morning;
  great is your faithfulness.
I say to myself, "The Lord is my portion;
  therefore I will wait for him."

Chapter 8

The Flight of the Swans

The heron was a particularly precious blessing of the river but it was not the only one. Its waters held another special gift for me too: swans. They were occasionally to be spotted gliding along in the water on the Perth to Gleneagles leg of the journey and, whenever I saw them, I would enjoy their graceful beauty.

However, one day, when I was feeling particularly low, the train passed just as several of them took flight over the river. As they rose up, my heart lifted with them in response to their lightness of being and freedom. **The grace of joy broke over me** and I felt with it a promise that Sam too would rise again.

To be clear, I did not hear or interpret what I saw as God saying that Sam would suddenly walk again. It was not specific in that way. It was the assurance offered to us all that our lives will take flight when we place our hope and trust in God.

Isaiah 40:31

> *. . . but those who hope in the Lord*
> *will renew their strength.*
> *They will soar on wings like eagles;*
> *they will run and not grow weary,*
> *they will walk and not be faint.*

I never saw the swans take flight like that again. However, the joy released in me on that day echoed onwards audibly enough for me to remember and carry forward some of the power of that moment.

My experience of the swans also reminded me of something I had heard a senior Anglican clergyman from Cape Town in South Africa say on a visit to London in 1988. He had maintained that,

'Joy is not the absence of pain but the presence of God.'

The truth of this assertion was confirmed for me in the joy I had felt in the rising of the swans despite how heavy my heart had been immediately beforehand. It was also being reinforced with time in other ways as well.

I was not active in the church as I focused on our family after the accident. No one expected me to lead contemplative prayer sessions or host bible studies. However, I was still on the rota for doing the Scripture reading on a Sunday morning and my turn eventually came up. Although I did not have to, I decided I could manage to do this one small thing. James would take friends down to visit Sam and I would stay home with Andrew that Sunday and go to church.

I received the reading a few days before, read it over and thought no more of it until I stood before the congregation and began to read aloud the assigned passage from Romans 12:9–21 which includes the following:

Romans 12:12
Be joyful in hope, patient in affliction, faithful in prayer.

I had read these words beforehand in preparation without any reaction or thought to their specific relevance to me but, as I declared them to the congregation, I struggled to hold back the tears. They had become personal as the emotion in my voice clearly revealed to everyone there. It was unnerving to be so exposed and vulnerable as I said them but, as I realised later, this was a profound moment of consolation for me. In other words, God had been powerfully present to me both as I heard His guidance to me in the words and as I declared them back to Him as an expression of my own desire.

It was both an intimate and a public moment; given to me but also to everyone else there. I felt the entire congregation with me as I said the words; they could not literally say them for me but I knew they were holding me as I did so. God was close. They were close. I could see that joy, patience, and faithfulness were possible.

I experienced that moment in church as a gift from God. It was God's grace cascading over and through me. The tears held a sorrow but they also bore witness to God's touch and presence which holds the promise of joy.

REFLECTION: EXTRAVAGANT GRACE

My experience of God's grace that morning was special but it was not unique. God is pouring out His grace on us continually. In 2006, I wrote a reflection on the all-encompassing and extravagant nature of God's grace. Although the full reflection is given in Appendix 6, I would invite you to reflect on the few verses I have chosen below.

····➔

If any one of these verses draws you more than another, do follow that prompt and focus on that verse alone. Otherwise allow these verses to lead you in a prayer of response to God for His extravagant grace in your life.

Extravagant Grace

When hope rises in us with the dawning of each day and is kindled in us even through times of stress and duress, *we have been graced, gifted, with hope.*

✠

When we feel our hearts burn with the awareness of God's presence, when we remember that we are never alone even though we may stand alone, *we have been graced, gifted, with consolation.*

✠

When we hear our name spoken and we recognise the voice of the one who calls us beloved, *we have been graced, gifted, with joy.*

✠

When our hearts know rest even when our lives are full of turmoil and strife, *we have been graced, gifted, with peace.*

✠

When in times of challenge we receive the love, comfort and encouragement of family and friends, *we have been graced, gifted, with the compassion of God offered through others.*

✠

If the train journey down to Glasgow held daily blessing which helped me to hold the pain I felt for Sam, the journey home for the first few months of 2010 was in a deep darkness which often chimed with my tiredness and sense of depletion at the end of the day. However, gradually the days began to lengthen; spring would not be held back. The evening journey home, both literally and emotionally, ceased to be through the long tunnel of night. The cold grasp of winter was unclenching its constraining hold on the land; green shoots of new growth and spring flowers were appearing and spreading. The paralysis was also slowly releasing some of its hold on Sam.

Sam had arrived in Glasgow still manifesting the paralysing effects of the inflammation the injury had caused to his spinal cord. Below the shoulders, he could move nothing. However, as the days slowly unfolded, the swelling subsided and we began to see some recovery in movement.

It did not happen all at once. I would arrive one day and discover that he could wiggle the toes on his right foot. Then a few days later it would be the whole of the right foot that was moving up and down. Doctors gradually discerned some movement higher up in the right leg. The right arm also improved as to some extent did the left, although much less strongly. We found ourselves naming the fingers on Sam's right hand as they began to show signs of some movement. In the left hand, although there was a hint of movement up towards the pinkie, there was no more than that. Similarly in the left leg, they could discern only the faintest flickers in the muscles, not enough to deliver functional benefit.

Sam's awareness of surface touch began to return too. It was altered but present more or less throughout his body. His ability to distinguish blunt versus sharp impacts recovered here and there as well, although it remained very patchy below the shoulders.

Every change made the heart leap and hope surge. However, the doctors had been brutally honest from day one and made clear that we had to anticipate that, whilst there could be positive changes, it was most likely that Sam would never walk again and would remain tetraplegic. Conflicting emotions had to cohabit. Hope encouraged a positive outlook and supported the gruelling and demanding daily rehabilitation work Sam had to do to make the very most of every improvement. Acceptance of what simply was had to find space too. Complete recovery was ultimately unlikely, and learning new ways of doing things with the limited function that did return was necessary.

Most days when I arrived in the unit, Sam was simply shattered. However, he was seldom negative or downcast. The first time I saw him express dismay was when, having spoken to the college in Oxford about what had happened, we had established that they would still take Sam so long as he met his conditions of two 'A' grades in his Advanced Higher exams. They were willing to let him defer sitting those exams for a year. I arrived believing this to be very good news but Sam was not impressed. He desperately wanted to move on and he did not want to sit his exams a year late. He was adamant that he would sit them that year if in hospital.

His consultant did not think this was advisable. He explained that it took at least six months for the body to recover at the most basic level from the sheer trauma of the accident to which the rehabilitation work only added further exhaustion. He would have little energy left over for the necessary study, never mind the concentration required for the actual exams. Sam, though, was determined. He would channel his efforts to what was needed. He would focus on preparing two Advanced Highers as required. He would sit French and Maths in May.

I had the skills to help him with the French. James teamed up with a close friend of Sam's to cover the Maths.[†] Sam's teachers, meanwhile, advised us on the syllabus requirements and of the various deadlines and hoops he had to move through prior to the exams.

It was a blessing that we could help Sam and were not dependent on external tutors. He was still doing all his rehabilitation physiotherapy with the result that, more often than not, we arrived to find him too tired to do very much at all. It didn't matter. We had at least four hours with him every day and could be flexible. We would snatch moments here and there when his energy had recovered enough to do some work. As we got closer to the exams, the hospital excused Sam from a couple of his physiotherapy sessions each week so that he had more time when he was not exhausted to learn and study.

Sam's studies were an added demand on him but they were also

[†]Sam's friend Laurie was studying at the University of Strathclyde in Glasgow and had sat Advanced Higher Maths the year before. He also visited Sam, almost daily, over the months he was in the spinal unit and played a huge role supporting him not just with his studies but, as a true friend would do, by simply being there.

a lifeline moving him forward in a positive way. He was not in doubt about the trajectory of his life. The next step was still clear. He was still going to leave home, eventually.

However, first he had to get home. Early in the year, after discussion with Sam, his medical team had agreed to his goal of getting home on weekend pass by the beginning of May in time for his school prom. To achieve this, the main adaptations our house would need would have to be started quickly and care arrangements would have to be sorted out sooner rather than later. Before long the necessary steps were being taken to move us towards this aim.

These preparations were not easy for me. I had to forge new relationships with Occupational Therapists, Care Managers and Social Workers and, in the process, I had to confront the fundamental reality and implications of what it would mean for Sam to live with the injury within the context of his home life and not just the hospital. Hard though it was, God's goodness and provision were apparent here too. Some of the professionals we were working with locally knew us already from church. I don't believe this afforded us preferential treatment but it was nonetheless deeply comforting to me to be known and even more so that Sam was known to them too.

REFLECTION: TO BE TRULY KNOWN

It is a great gift, a joy, to be truly known; to feel safe enough with someone to be fully revealed before them.

I would invite you to contemplate John 20:10–16 which tells the story of Jesus appearing to Mary Magdalene after the crucifixion for the first time.

I would encourage you to notice especially the joy in Mary's voice when she recognises the voice of the One who knows her and speaks her name. Imagine the joy that Jesus might have felt too when He is recognised in turn.

✠

Centre, Read, Contemplate, Review, Journal

Prayers for Sam's healing were constant and yet despite the gains each month brought, the fundamental picture did not change. As his recovery began to plateau, he was heading towards being discharged from the unit in July 2010 as a disabled person. You might conclude that our prayers were not being heard and not being answered. However, although we were not getting to witness the joy of Sam walking out of the unit, we were ultimately witnessing something just as remarkable, if not more so.

Sam's spirits remained strong. He showed exceptional strength and maturity in his fortitude and forbearance. His attitude was a daily miracle. Although paralysed in body, he was not obviously constrained in spirit and that made him, in a way, less paralysed than those of us for whom fear and despair, regret and anger, bitterness and sorrow act as brakes and limits on how we engage our lives.

I don't know how to break down the constituent parts to tell you on what Sam's resolve was based.

📖 How much of his courage and resilience came from the personality he was born with?

📖 How significant was the love he had grown up with?

📖 How important were the visits, support, and love of his family and friends?

📖 Was it the prayers of the many who surrounded us or the faith he had always been surrounded by and nurtured himself that kept him confident of his future?

📖 How much difference was made by the blessing of good roommates at the spinal unit to share the ups and the downs with?

📖 What was contributed by the professionals at the unit who encouraged him and worked to support his recovery?

📖 Was it just the irrepressible optimism of youth or the fact that he had just had the offer from Oxford only three days prior to the accident that gave him hope?

I cannot possibly know what did what. I do know that Sam's response to his situation was a grace for him and a grace for us and, as I was on the lookout for it, revealed for me the active presence of God with him. Sam had a powerful companion; One who could and would equip him daily to live this altered life; One who could make him fly.

In the hospital chapel seven months earlier, God had invited me to live with and through the pain the accident had caused for us all. My heart needed to remain open in its tender and hurt state so that He could minister His healing love to me. I needed to be awake so that I would see that love coming to me in tangible and physical ways; through our families, friends, the church, and all the people who would play their part in helping us to step through the implications of Sam's injury.

There was no detail too small for God's attention. I felt His hand upon it all. He revealed His goodness as a Shepherd. As I had hoped and believed, He came now more than ever as Saviour and Redeemer who could and would transform this experience for good. That transformation might not happen overnight but slowly and surely, if we let God work, golden threads would be continually woven into this experience.

My contemplative journey over the previous years is what had laid down the foundations of my confidence in God and had prepared me to hear His invitation and to trust it.

It is through contemplation more than any other discipline that I personally have learnt to listen for His voice. When I have wandered and lost sight of Him, it helps me to recognise that voice again, to turn and follow Him back.

It is the tool He gave me to take me from the place of exhaustion in 1997 via the open expanse of the desert to greener pastures with still waters.

However, contemplative prayer is not some kind of 'wonder discipline' that presto fixes everything. It is not an answer; it is a way to deepen our relationship with God who can enable us to live the day that is given.

God longs for us to be awake to His presence so that He can bless us, as repeatedly promised in Scripture, with love, peace, hope, and joy. Contemplative prayer encourages us to be attentive, to be alert, and to be expectant; indeed to be like herons looking out for and waiting on His provision.

When I first stepped out to share the benefits of contemplative prayer with others in Australia, it was because I knew already how much I gained from it. In the wake of the accident I am even more confident to say that it is worth a try. It is as simple as being prepared to stop, open to look, and willing to listen in God's presence. The blessings of hearing God are certain for He says:

Isaiah 55:3

Give ear and come to me;
* listen, that you may live.*

Finally, contemplative prayer has taught me to expect God's presence in all the moments of my life; both the ordinary and extraordinary ones. Spotting Him by my side and by the side of my fellow pilgrims so often over the years is what gave me courage when I really needed it. It enabled me to lay aside my fears, to endure the pain, and to trust that He could take me not just through the valley but, when everything would suggest otherwise, He would enable me to go on the heights.

In the words of Habakkuk:

Habakkuk 3:17–19:

Though the fig tree does not bud
* and there are no grapes on the vines,*
though the olive crop fails
* and the fields produce no food,*
though there are no sheep in the pen
* and no cattle in the stalls,*
yet I will rejoice in the Lord,
* I will be joyful in God my Saviour.*
The Sovereign Lord is my strength;

he makes my feet like the feet of a deer,
he enables me to tread on the heights.

Indeed seven years on, Sam is not walking. Like the heron, we wait. However, like the swans, Sam has nonetheless taken flight.

Epilogue

We had our accident on the 21st December 2009 and, after an operation to stabilise his neck, Sam was transferred a week later from the Aberdeen Royal Infirmary to the Queen Elizabeth II National Spinal Injuries Unit in Glasgow to continue his recovery and rehabilitation.

Sam had his first visit home on pass at the start of May 2010, as hoped, in time for his 6th year school prom.

Two weeks later he sat his Advanced Higher Maths and French exams in hospital. He was allowed extra time for both exams as they were being scribed for him; three hour exams became five hour marathons. Prior to the exams, I had not seen Sam able to concentrate on his studies for more than two hours at a stretch. A lot of prayer for his physical energy and stamina surrounded him through both exam sessions.

Sam passed both exams with the requisite 'A' grades to enable him to take up his place at Merton College, Oxford. In fact, he achieved the highest exam result in Scotland for his French paper. He received, as a result, the Franco-Scottish Society's Lansdowne Award for this achievement. It was the first time in the 25 years since the award had been established that a student from a state school had won the prize.

To allow Merton College the time to make the necessary

adaptations to its facilities, it was agreed that Sam would matriculate to begin his degree in October 2011. Sam had a gap year to fill.

Sam was discharged from the unit in Glasgow on the 27th July 2010. He came out with a spinal cord injury that categorised him as tetraplegic with the recovery already detailed on pages 143 and 144. However, although ready for discharge, spinal patients can continue to experience improvements in their condition for up to five years. Sam recovered movement in his left wrist in January 2011, a significant gain for him, and has year on year gained in strength through his arms and core especially.

Every little bit of recovery has a benefit. Sam's fingers on his right hand, for example, do not have strong movement but he has a good enough grip with his index finger and thumb to enable him to eat independently, to hold a pen and write, and to manage all the usual forms of modern technology such as mobile phones, tablets, and computers.

He was discharged with an electric wheelchair. However, his level of recovery made a manual wheelchair with electric wheels – an e-motion wheelchair – an option. Today he has both but most often uses his manual chair. Batteries in the hubs of the wheels provide power to give extra support to each thrust Sam gives. The chair collapses and the wheels can be removed for travelling.

When Sam left hospital he was dependent on a hoist to transfer from his chair to his bed. However, he had been shown how to do assisted transfers meaning that, with a sliding sheet, a simple transfer board, and some help, he could move from one surface to another. As Sam's core continued to strengthen, he became increasingly competent and able to transfer without the use of a hoist and with minimal help. Today he has the option of the hoist or not and chooses one over the other depending on the circumstances. He is also able to do assisted transfers in and out of the front seat of a car.

Sam requires support with his personal needs and someone available to him at all other times to provide assistance when required. Before Sam was discharged from the unit, James and I made sure that we had been fully trained in how to provide the assistance he needed. To begin with, we had external carers providing help in the mornings following which I took over. However, once Sam went to Oxford, he had the full-time support of a Personal Assistant (PA) during term whilst, over the holidays, I continued to provide this cover. Since leaving home, my role has ceased but the full-time support of a PA has continued.

We had our first family holiday in the August of 2010; just weeks after Sam had been discharged. We stayed in adapted self-catering accommodation in Ayrshire for a week just 50 miles from the unit; nice and close to help should anything have gone wrong. A few months later we went further and stayed for a week near Oxford while we met with the university to discuss Sam's needs and the adaptations he would require to his rooms.

Long before Sam was discharged, I had begun to wonder if it might be possible to take advantage of his gap year to do a big trip. I wanted him to feel that his world had not shrunk but, if differently, he could still do many exciting things. In January 2011, 7 months after discharge, Sam and I undertook a 6 week holiday to New Zealand and Australia to meet up with and visit friends as well as seeing some new places.

Over the course of the holiday, we took 9 separate flights. We slept in 14 hotels/motels/units. We covered close to 2,000 miles by car and 20,000 miles by plane. This was possible at this early stage because of three factors, in particular:

- 📖 I was able to provide Sam's care
- 📖 he could do assisted transferring enabling him to get in and out of an ordinary car and on and off of beds with relative ease without the need of a hoist
- 📖 his e-motion wheelchair was small enough, once collapsed, to go in the back of a car[†]

It was an exhausting holiday for both of us but an exhilarating one and gave us a sense of all that was still possible. God is good.

Since then we have continued to travel just as we would have done previously, taking annual holidays in France, visiting friends in England, The Netherlands, the United States, and so on. We often have to stay in hotels where access and provision can vary in standard. I do as much homework as possible to choose the best possible facilities for us but, even when well-prepared, we can arrive to find that things are not quite right. In those instances, we have learnt to adapt and to find a way round any problems. It is worth mentioning here that I have nearly always found that people want to help us; there is so much kindness and goodwill, more than we often realise.

During Sam's gap year, for all that he had said he did not want to go back to school, he did. When at home, he went in regularly to help his French teacher and he prepared for and sat Higher Italian in which he got an 'A' grade.

[†]It can be possible to hire equipment and wheelchair accessible vehicles when abroad. However, it is much easier and less expensive not to have to.

After some hunting on the internet, I found a company that make excellent jeans specifically for people who are wheelchair-bound. Sam has as many pairs of jeans as before, if not more.

Sam began his degree in Philosophy, Politics and Economics in October 2011. He sat his final exams in June 2014. These were again 5 hour marathons. However, this time, he was able to write them himself, and achieve a 2:1 in the process.

As a family we watch with interest the developments in spinal injury research. Sam was seventeen when his injury occurred; the hope and prayer is that the breakthrough we all long for will come while he is still young and fit. However, Sam is not living dependent on that outcome. He is living the life he has. He is living today. There is a contemplative prayer session in that wisdom!

When Sam left hospital in 2010, members of our church and friends offered to continue praying for Sam. Nehemiah had rebuilt the walls of Jerusalem with the help of many and so we would pray for Sam's rebuilding muscle by muscle. All his key muscle groups were listed and people signed up to pray for them, many continue to do so. We will be 'faithful in prayer' and wait for Sam's full recovery.

As a family we have journeyed together through this experience. It had implications for each one of us. There are more stories which could be told but so far, for me, they can be summarised in the flight of the swans and the profound wisdom that Joy is not the absence of pain but the presence of God.

May Joy find you and bless you too.

Sam and I, 2014

Appendix 1

A Reflection on Roots: The Karri Tree

When I lived in Perth, Western Australia, I used to love visiting the south west of the state with its beautiful coastline, limestone caves, and towering trees. The Karri trees, in particular, stood out for me because not only did they grow to amazing heights of up to 90 metres or more – Big Ben standing at 96 metres puts that in context – but they also had impressive root structures which could actually be seen when visiting some of the caves. Indeed the Karri puts down a vast network of vertical and horizontal roots in search of the water and nutrients it needs and can drill through metre upon metre of rock, if necessary, to reach the water table below.

As Christians, we are called to live our lives deeply rooted in God so that we might be nourished and strengthened by His Word and action in our lives and so that we might stand up and out as witnesses of His love and compassion for us and the world Jesus died for.

I would invite you to reflect on your own root structure and growth as you consider these verses from Jeremiah:

Jeremiah 17: 7–8

But blessed is the one who trusts in the Lord,
*   whose confidence is in him.*
They will be like a tree planted by the water
*   that sends out its roots by the stream.*

It does not fear when heat comes;
   its leaves are always green.
It has no worries in a year of drought
   and never fails to bear fruit.

How and from where do you draw sustenance?

Are you adequately resourced at all times regardless of circumstances?

✠

Finish by reviewing this time of prayer. Notice any thoughts, feelings, or words that particularly struck you as you reflected. Allow these to lead you in a prayer of response to God.

Appendix 2

The Contemplation of Our Daily Lives

We can live very busy and demanding lives which can make it hard to notice as it is happening all the ways God is announcing His presence with us and perhaps seeking to comfort, guide or challenge us. As a result, it is worthwhile to set aside time regularly to look back in search of where God might have been. We can reflect back over any time period: the day just finishing, the week past, the month past, the year past, or any other timeframe we choose. The more frequently we do this, the better.

This discipline, associated with the spirituality of St Ignatius of Loyola and his **Daily Examen of Consciousness**, can help us not only to identify those moments which are alive with God's presence versus those that are not but will also help us to uncover any patterns in our behaviour or relationships which lead us towards or away from God. In both cases, the benefit is discernment which we can apply to the choices in our lives. We want more of those moments that are full of God and less of those that are not.

It is important to ask and trust God's Holy Spirit to guide our prayer and reflection when we do this else we might choose to ignore or discount moments that are actually full of God; either because we don't rate them as being holy enough or because they disturb us in some way.

Below is a step by step example of how you might approach this type of contemplation. You can contemplate any period but this example focuses on yesterday. If you plan to do this now, I would suggest reading through the whole process first so you know what to expect and then come back and begin.

Step 1: Centring

Start by taking a few moments to settle yourself into prayer. You can focus on your breathing and/or you could choose a simple phrase or word to repeat and to which you can return if you find your attention wandering as you pray such as 'Come Holy Spirit, Come'.

✠

Step 2: Discerning God's Presence

When you feel settled, invite the Holy Spirit to bring to your attention those moments over yesterday for which you feel most grateful, those times when you felt most alive, or perhaps full of peace, love, hope or joy, or close to God in some other way. These are moments that may, but not necessarily, shine or stand out positively for you.

✠

Invite the Holy Spirit to clarify why those moments come to mind. They may be moments referred to as ones of *consolation* because they were full of God's presence. As you listen out for the Holy Spirit's response, experience again what those moments held for you.

✠

Step 3: Discerning When You Have Missed God's Presence

Then invite the Holy Spirit to show you any moments when you felt distant from God or others around you; times when you felt out of step with God's Spirit, off kilter or drained of energy. These might be low moments or ones when you felt angry or sad, although challenging emotions do not automatically mean we are distant from God. You may even have experienced what is known as *desolation*; a feeling of God's absence.

✠

Do not be tempted to judge those moments but ask the Holy Spirit to help you understand what made those moments hard. Was it something that was said or something that was done or not done? The invitation here is not to move immediately to fix what is past but, by being present to the insight it holds, to be able to carry that wisdom as you go forward. As you remain present to the discomfort of those moments, invite God to fill you with the love, mercy, hope, peace or other grace that you might need.

✠

Step 4: Give Thanks

As you conclude your prayer time, give thanks for what has been received.

✠

Step 5: Journal

Finally keep a record of what you have experienced as, over time, this is how patterns will be revealed that will help you to recognise where God is present in your life thus guiding and helping you, as a result, to make better choices.

✠

Appendix 3

The Contemplation of God

The contemplation of God is the silent waiting on God which I expect, for most of us, would seem the most daunting form of contemplation. We come before the living but invisible God echoing the hope and confidence of David when he said, 'Truly my soul finds rest in God.'[†] However, the gazing that has anchored our attention when considering Creation, an object, a scripture, or our lives is not so simple with God, who cannot be whipped out of our pockets for easy observation.

When our contemplation is of God alone, He is nevertheless the focus of our intent as we come offering ourselves and our presence to Him. We are before Him just as we are. We wait and we listen. We trust in His divine presence. We cannot dwell in the presence of the living God and come away unchanged; we will be transformed by the encounter. We reflect after on how we were touched by the prayer time as we treasure the gifts of that time with God.

Contemplating God in silence becomes easier with practice. Therefore, start small by sitting for only short lengths of time in contemplation and gradually build from there. I would suggest you begin by doing so for just five minutes – consider setting an alarm to go at the end of the five minutes if you have one to hand. Then

---

†Psalm 62:1

read this through before you start so that, once you do begin, you will not need to refer to it again during your time of contemplation.

The suggestions here for entering into the time of contemplation are only suggestions. Pray as you can. In other words, if something hinders rather than helps you to contemplate, feel free to ignore it. Do what works best for you. This is always true whatever the contemplative exercise.

Step 1: Centring

I would suggest you begin by paying attention to your posture. Sit comfortably and let the chair fully hold your weight but such that you remain erect and alert. You may find it helpful to have both feet planted firmly on the ground. This will help to stabilise your posture.

You might like to rest your hands on your lap with your palms up. It will give physical expression to any desire to come in surrender before God; offering yourself wholly to Him and open to receive from Him.

✠

As in previous contemplations, I would encourage you to take a couple of minutes to focus on your breath or to use the technique of repeating a phrase or a word to help you settle.

If you choose to focus on your breath, you might like to imagine that with each inhalation of your breath you are drawing closer to God and with each exhalation you are letting go of that which distracts you or takes your attention away.

✠

Step 2: Contemplating God

When you are ready, imagine yourself sitting with God.

It may help you to anchor your presence in the silence, if you imagine a setting for this encounter. You might like to visualise a throne room like that depicted in Revelation 4. Alternatively, you could picture the less imposing setting of a homestead and being with God as the parent who longs for our presence as described in the parable of the Prodigal Son.[†] As you sit with God, be attentive to Him in the silence.

✠

If you find your thoughts wandering, simply focus again on your breathing, or the phrase or word you used as you began then carry on again from there.

✠

Step 3: Review

At the end of the five minutes, reflect on how it felt.

Don't be put off having another go if you are not sure there was any immediate benefit. Trust that God will delight in your time with Him in this way. Over time and with practice, you will find you can sit in silence more naturally and for longer.

✠

Step 4: Journal

Make a note in your journal of any particular thoughts or feelings that arise from your contemplation.

✠

†Luke 15:11–32

Appendix 4

The Contemplation of Scripture

Out of the Ordinary: The Woman at the Well

Outlined below is a contemplation of the gospel story of the woman at the well found in John 4 which I scripted for a retreat in 2009 followed by a poem which I also wrote at that time. This guided contemplation expands the story but remains faithful to its essential details. You could choose to contemplate this story as it is offered here or you could read it through as an example of the contemplative process but focus on working through the biblical narrative in your own way as you feel the Holy Spirit leading you.

Step 1: Centring

Begin by taking some time to focus on your posture and your breath. Settle yourself comfortably but so as to remain alert as you become aware of the rhythm of your breathing. Draw close to God with each breath in and let go gently of that which distracts you and would draw you away as you breathe out. You might like to take up the words 'Living Water' and slowly repeat them to deepen your focus as you settle.

Step 2: Read the Passage at Least Twice
John 4: 4–15

Now he had to go through Samaria. So he came to a town in

Samaria called Sychar, near the plot of ground Jacob had given to his son Joseph. Jacob's well was there, and Jesus, tired as he was from the journey, sat down by the well. It was about noon.

When a Samaritan woman came to draw water, Jesus said to her, "Will you give me a drink?" (His disciples had gone into the town to buy food.)

The Samaritan woman said to him, "You are a Jew and I am a Samaritan woman. How can you ask me for a drink?" (For Jews do not associate with Samaritans.)

Jesus answered her, "If you knew the gift of God and who it is that asks you for a drink, you would have asked him and he would have given you living water."

"Sir," the woman said, "you have nothing to draw with and the well is deep. Where can you get this living water? Are you greater than our father Jacob, who gave us the well and drank from it himself, as did also his sons and his livestock?"

Jesus answered, "Everyone who drinks this water will be thirsty again, but whoever drinks the water I give them will never thirst. Indeed, the water I give them will become in them a spring of water welling up to eternal life."

The woman said to him, "Sir, give me this water so that I won't get thirsty and have to keep coming here to draw water."

Step 3: Contemplation of the Passage

You can either use the guided contemplation written below or you can enter into the scene picturing it in all its detail as you feel the Holy Spirit leading you. Take your time either way allowing the

Holy Spirit to guide the pace and length of what you do.

Guided Contemplation

Let us picture the scene: you are at home, it is midday, the sun outside is beating down overhead and you are preparing to go and draw water from the well. This is your daily routine. You go when things are quiet, when the other women are away having drawn their water earlier in the cool of the day. You were not and are not welcome among them, you know that. It is a long and complicated story but the bottom line is simple – five husbands and a live-in partner later and women like you are rewarded – or is that punished? – with the strength-sapping heat of the midday sun for your choices. Do you blame them? Perhaps if things were different you would do the same to a woman like you.

✠

You are used to it and, with resignation, you pick up your bucket and set off. The well is some distance from your home and you walk down one street and then another, your body takes these turns without the slightest hesitation. You could do it in your sleep; you know this walk so well. You step into whatever shadows you can find with the deep-set knowledge of how the sun falls over the town at this time of day. It is hot, oh so hot. It is also quiet. A few more streets and you will be there.

✠

Is your mind wandering, lost in thought and oblivious to everything? After all is there any need to be alert and attentive when you do this every day? You hear of things happening elsewhere and to other people but not here, not in this town, not to you – each day is the same, what hope could steal its way in and surprise you – it is usually someone sticking out their foot to trip you up, so is it better head down and on with what has to be done?

✠

You round the corner to where the well sits and a foot catches the upper end of your vision. What is this? A man sitting by the well at midday and a Jew at that! Oh, this could be a bother, how do you navigate getting your water as though he were not there? You are just pondering this question when he speaks to you and asks *you* for water! You nearly fall over. What was it you were thinking earlier, head down and watch out for the foot that will trip you up? You were right.

✠

He is a Jew and he is asking you, a Samaritan woman, for help, for water. How can that be? Everyone knows, don't they, that Jews and Samaritans don't mix? Still, you can point out to him that you know this even if he doesn't seem to know what is right and proper.

✠

However, that has not shut him up; not at all. Now you are confused because he is suggesting that if you knew who he was, *you* should have asked *him* for water and he would have given you *living* water. What does he mean? He has no bucket, just how was he going to do that? You wonder if the heat is getting to both of you so you ask him a few well-chosen questions and make clear whose well this was: none other than *the* Jacob's. Indeed, none other than Jacob himself had built it, drunk from it, and used it for his flocks and herds. That would put some perspective on things, you may not know a lot but that should put things in context here.

✠

But no, this water he says will not ultimately satisfy or slay your thirst. He says that he would give you water such that you would never be thirsty again, water that will be *in* you, *in* you like a spring, gurgling and bubbling up to eternal life. What can this mean? Where is this water? What is this water and how do you get to it? You look at him and you look at your bucket. You look at the well and you close your eyes.

You see the well that you have come to every day, every day for as long as you can remember. It is deep, so deep and the water that you pull up from it is so cool, so refreshing, so restorative, and so vital. You picture a space deep within you like this well. Down, down, down you go, you lower your bucket deep into yourself, waiting for the splosh as the bucket hits the water.

How far do you have to go? How far do you have to be willing to go? How much dirt and rock must be cleared away as you go? He says that it will well up in you. How abundant is it? Does the bucket overflow? Indeed, do you even need the bucket? And how much do *you* desire this water, this cool, refreshing, restorative and vital water that he promises will rise up within you always?

At the Well

It was in the heat of the day
weary from Your road
that You stopped by the water.

She came to fill up
for the hour and day ahead
from this, Jacob's well.

How could she have been ready
for this encounter?
A place of daily toil
become holy and sacred space.

Water asked for
and water given.
Water promised for every hour
and day ahead.

How could she have been ready
for this encounter?
The lonely place
become holy and sacred space.

How deep was the well?
How far did the bucket have to fall?
How much effort to make it surface?

How costly is this encounter
when the ordinary is full of grace?
When our lives have become
the holy and sacred space.

Step 4: Review

Take time now to review your time of prayer noticing where you may have felt the Holy Spirit stirring in you as you prayed. Allow this to lead your prayer of response and give thanks for what you have received.

✠

Step 5: Journal

Gather up your thoughts from your time of review and journal these so that you have a record you can refer back to as appropriate.

✠

Appendix 5

A Contemplative Prayer Session

What follows is an example of one of my contemplative prayer sessions.

Session Title:

JESUS ASKS, "WHO DO YOU SAY I AM?"

Exercise 1: Centring *(5–10 minutes)*

Begin by focusing on your breath. Take deep and slow breaths and, as you do so, allow your weight with each exhalation to root you more firmly in your chair. Let the chair hold all your weight just as God holds you in being.

As you lean into God, open your hands and place them palms up on your lap. Continue to breathe deeply as you slowly and silently repeat for a time the invitation, 'Come Holy Spirit, Come.'

Then continue to sit before God in the silence. Be at rest and at peace in his presence. If you feel yourself drifting, simply take up again the phrase of invitation, 'Come Holy Spirit, Come'.

☩

Exercise 2 *(20 minutes)*

In Psalm 46:10, God says: '**Be still, and know that I am God**.' Below are eleven statements which summarise who the Lord is for the psalmist, based on the indicated psalms. Sit with each of these in turn allowing any imagery they evoke to bless or challenge you as God leads. Finish with the verse from Psalm 63, allowing it to lead you in a prayer of response to God.

Psalm 11: The Lord is my Refuge

Psalm 23: The Lord is my Shepherd

Psalm 27: The Lord is my Salvation

Psalm 27: The Lord is my Light

Psalm 28: The Lord is my Rock

Psalm 46: The Lord is my Strength

Psalm 59: The Lord is my Deliverer

Psalm 69: The Lord is my Saviour

Psalm 90: The Lord is my Dwelling Place

Psalm 93: The Lord is my King

Psalm 121: The Lord is my Helper

Psalm 63:1:

You, God, are my God

✠

Exercise 3 *(30 minutes)*

You are invited to **contemplate** the passage below taken from *The Message* version of the bible. Take time to enter into the scene and to be present to what is happening from one of the perspectives of the story.

Mark 8: 27–29

Jesus and his disciples headed out for the villages around Caesarea Philippi. As they walked, he asked, "Who do the people say I am?"

"Some say 'John the Baptiser,'" they said. "Others say 'Elijah.' Still others say 'one of the prophets.'"

He then asked, "And you—what are you saying about me? Who am I?"

Peter gave the answer: "You are the Christ, the Messiah."

✠

When you have finished contemplating this passage of Scripture, review your prayer time considering the two questions below if you have not already done so:

📖 Who do you say Jesus is?
📖 Who is Jesus for you today?

✠

Give thanks for what you have received.

✠

Finish by taking a moment to **journal** any insights.

✠

Appendix 6

A Reflection on the Extravagant Grace of God

When hope rises in us with the dawning of each day and is kindled in us even through times of stress and duress, *we have been graced, gifted, with hope.*

✠

When we feel our hearts burn with the awareness of God's presence, when we remember that we are never alone even though we may stand alone, *we have been graced, gifted, with consolation.*

✠

When we hear our name spoken and we recognise the voice of the one who calls us beloved, *we have been graced, gifted, with joy.*

✠

When our hearts know rest even when our lives are full of turmoil and strife, *we have been graced, gifted, with peace.*

✠

When we remember Christ saying "It is finished" on the cross, *we have been graced, gifted, with reconciliation.*

✠

When in times of challenge we receive the love, comfort, and encouragement of family and friends, *we have been graced, gifted, with the compassion of God offered through others.*

✠

When we remember the orphans and the widows in our deeds as well as our words; when we love the stranger in our midst and care for the refugee and the outcast, *we have been graced, gifted, with the heart of the Samaritan and a thirst for God's justice.*

✠

When we lose our way making choices that lead us towards the darkness of the tomb and yet hear the voice of Christ calling us to come out into the light, *we have been graced, gifted, with a forgiveness that sets us free to shed the grave clothes and claim life.*

✠

When we consider that the sun shines and the rain falls freely on all mankind whether good or evil; when we remember our own mistakes, past, present, and to come which helped to drive the nails into Jesus on the cross; when gratitude not judgement rises up within us then we have beheld the extraordinary and overwhelming mercy that flows out to us again and again, and *we have been graced, gifted, with humility before our Saviour, and a path of peace and forgiveness to tread towards our enemies.*

✠

When good choices are made instead of bad ones; when generosity replaces avarice and greed; when we are slow to anger, and patience governs our thoughts and deeds, *we have been graced, gifted, with God's discernment in action.*

✠

When we find in ourselves talent and ability, and with them the courage to step out and be ourselves, *we have been graced, gifted, with God's loving attention in our making and living.*

✠

When our hearts are stirred by beauty; when the bees dance in the wildflowers; when we hear the symphony of birdsong above the breeze; when we look up at the heavens late at night and see the stars set like diamonds in a cathedral ceiling, *we have been graced, gifted, with awe before the majesty of Creation.*

✠

When we tread lightly in this world considering what we need to live rather than all we want; when we ponder the incredible wealth of the earth's provision, *we have been graced, gifted, with God's love and respect for the world He created.*

✠

When breakthroughs are made through research; when archaeology reveals history and insights into the past; when frontiers in space are explored uncovering new horizons and opportunities, *we have been graced, gifted, with a thirst for knowledge and understanding, and with curiosity rewarded.*

✠

When the great masters of music, art, and theatre reveal to us in new ways the world around us, *we have been graced, gifted, with creativity and its wisdom which helps us to make new connections and reach deeper levels of desire for our creator God.*

✠

When we recognise that everything, absolutely everything, comes from the God who loves us and calls us beloved; when we open our hands to receive from Him each day what we need, giving thanks that we worship a God who did not consider any cost too great to draw us to Himself; when we remember that nothing we do can make Him love us more or make Him love us less; when we acknowledge His outrageously extravagant gifts, *we have indeed been graced, gifted, with a story to share with others.*

✠

Amen

Appendix 7

Frequently Asked Questions

The following questions are addressed in this section:
1. What is the difference between meditation and contemplation?
2. How do I know whether what I have heard is of God or not?
3. When should I do contemplative prayer?
4. Can you recommend other sources on this subject?

1. What is the difference between meditation and contemplation?

Meditation is a word associated with many different spiritual traditions. Its exact meaning and use can vary accordingly. The way I use the word meditation distinguishes it from contemplation.

Meditation also has a powerful and transformative potential but through a process which emphasises the active work of the mind as we endeavour to understand better the full meaning of the object of our focus. In this context, it is an intellectual process of engagement with Scripture; we chew on, wrestle and grapple with its meaning and application in our lives. As we do so, the words with their truth and revelation take deeper root in us thereby transforming our hearts and minds.

The difference might be best understood in this way: in contemplation, it is not that we ignore our intellects but, as we linger and focus on whatever is before us, we receive from it with open and gentle hands. By comparison, in meditation, as we hold God's Word, we are busy with those hands teasing the text apart in order to understand its relevance and meaning better. Contemplation might ultimately flow into meditation and meditation may become contemplation. They are very closely linked but, in my view, different.

2. How do I know whether what I have heard is of God or not?

This is an important question as not everything we may think or feel necessarily comes from God. This is why it is so crucial to review the time of prayer and, particularly so, when we feel moved to take some kind of action. At such times, I have found these next questions and suggestions especially helpful for discernment.

• Do I feel driven or do I feel drawn?

God never coerces us. His call to us to follow Him is always an invitation. He leaves us free to choose whether we will do so or not. His voice is quiet and gentle; one that **draws us** to Him and to His purposes for us. It is a voice that calls us towards fullness of life; that sets us free; that is merciful. If we do not respond, God can be trusted to call us again. He is insistent but He is not aggressive.

The voice that is not of God is often, by comparison, loud. It shouts in our ear. It plays on emotions like guilt. It compels and drives us to actions or towards responses that will keep us captive and not set us free. It is often an accusing voice and full of deceit, encouraging us to acts that look righteous but are not.

- **Does this lead to greater faith, hope, and love?**

  We have a formidable and devious foe. We need to be able to spot the wolf in sheep's clothing. This question about faith, hope, and love is very helpful to that end. Paul tells us in 1 Corinthians 13:13 that faith, hope, and love are what remain when the imperfect disappears. They are like hallmarks on silver, they attest to God's presence. If they are absent from or undermined by our response or action then we can anticipate that God was not present in what we thought we heard.

- **Is this consistent with the work of the Holy Spirit?**

  In Galatians 5:25 we are encouraged to keep in step with the Spirit. The fruit of the Spirit is love, joy, peace, patience, kindness, goodness, faithfulness, gentleness and self-control. The presence or absence of these attributes of the Spirit is also helpful as we seek to discern if what we have heard in our contemplation is truly of God.

- **Allow time and remain attentive for God to confirm His prompting**

  Our world is in a hurry and the pressure is usually on to provide instant responses to everything. However, rushing often leads to poor choices. As Christians, we can trust God's timing. We can afford the time to wait on Him, if necessary. When might it be necessary though? I was once advised that we should HALT when we are experiencing any one or more of the feelings below:

  📖 **Hurried**

  📖 **Anxious**

📖 **Low**

📖 **Tired**

God can and will confirm His purposes. He can do this in any number of ways: through the words of others, through further reading, through the events of our lives, through the message of a sermon, and so on. God only needs us to allow Him the time to do so.

3. When should I do contemplative prayer?

The answer is that we can bring the contemplative gaze to all of our day; a looking and listening for God in and through everything. This is a dimension of *praying continually,* as already noted. There are tremendous riches to be uncovered in opening our eyes and ears to God's presence in this way.

We can also choose to use contemplation more intentionally alongside our other prayers. We may be reading a passage of Scripture that is particularly rich with imagery and so we choose to take our reading deeper using contemplation. We do not have to but it is a tool available to us at such times.

We may be seeking specific guidance over an issue in our lives and, although contemplating our day at the end of every day is beneficial, if we do not do it regularly, we may find it a useful discipline for a period as we seek discernment regarding that issue. Also, scriptures which lend themselves to contemplation may come to mind to aid that uncovering of God's will.

We may be drawn to contemplative prayer whether we have a specific benefit we wish to draw from it or not. We may simply wish to offer our presence to God. Our desire may echo that of the psalmist:

Psalm 27:4
One thing I ask of the Lord,
this is what I seek:
that I may dwell in the house of the Lord
all the days of my life,
to gaze upon the beauty of the Lord
and to seek him in his temple.

The riches of contemplative prayer are always available and accessible to us. The more we do it, the more we will be confident to do it and will, most likely, want to do it and know when it will help us.

4. Can you recommend other sources on this subject?

You may find the following writers helpful sources as you look to be more attentive to God. This is, of course, by no means an exhaustive list. Rather it reflects my taste and those who I find encourage me to keep alert and expectant as I journey.

Frederick Beuchner
Barbara Brown Taylor
Richard Foster
Sandra Holt
Gerard W. Hughes
Thomas Merton
Kathleen Norris
Henri Nouwen
Charles Ringma
Richard Rohr

Joyce Rupp
Margaret Silf
Philip Yancey

I would specifically recommend '*Sleeping with Bread*' by Dennis, Sheila and Matthew Lint if you wish to read further about the Daily Examen of Consciousness and the Ignatian practice of reviewing your day regularly in prayer.

Appendix 8

Paving Stones

I have listed below the many scriptures that were sent to me and from which I drew strength over the months Sam was in the spinal unit. On those days when the pain I felt was acute and my sorrow for Sam overwhelming, these verses were what kept me going as they encouraged me to keep my eyes on God and to trust Him. The verses are listed in the order they would appear in the bible rather than in an order of preference. They are also given in the form I received them and, therefore, from whatever translation of the bible that the sender used.

Some do have very special meaning for me. However, they were all gifts and played a role on the day that I received them and then carried them forward thereafter. Some I received repeatedly as different friends were moved to send them to me at different times.

Together they created a firm foundation on which to stand and walk.

Deuteronomy 31:6

Be strong and courageous. Do not be afraid or terrified because of them, for the Lord your God goes with you; he will never leave you nor forsake you.

Joshua 1:9

Have I not commanded you? Be strong and courageous. Do not be afraid; do not be discouraged, for the Lord your God will be with you wherever you go.

Psalm 3:4–6

I call out to the Lord,
*   and he answers me from his holy mountain.*
I lie down and sleep;
*   I wake again, because the Lord sustains me.*
I will not fear though tens of thousands
*   assail me on every side.*

Psalm 18:2

The Lord is my rock, my fortress and my deliverer;
*   my God is my rock, in whom I take refuge,*
*   my shield and the horn of my salvation, my stronghold.*

Psalm 18:28–29

You, Lord, keep my lamp burning;
*   my God turns my darkness into light.*
With your help I can advance against a troop;
*   with my God I can scale a wall.*

Psalm 22:4–5

In you our ancestors put their trust;
*   they trusted and you delivered them.*
To you they cried out and were saved;
*   in you they trusted and were not put to shame.*

Psalm 27:13–14

I remain confident of this:
  I will see the goodness of the Lord
  in the land of the living.
Wait for the Lord;
  be strong and take heart
  and wait for the Lord.

Psalm 34:7

The angel of the Lord encamps around those who fear him,
  and he delivers them.

Psalm 34:18

The Lord is close to the broken-hearted
  and saves those who are crushed in spirit.

Psalm 46:1–3

God is our refuge and strength,
  an ever-present help in trouble.
Therefore we will not fear, though the earth give way
  and the mountains fall into the heart of the sea,
though its waters roar and foam
  and the mountains quake with their surging.

Psalm 56:3–4

When I am afraid, I put my trust in you.
  In God, whose word I praise–
in God I trust and am not afraid.
  What can mere mortals do to me?

Psalm 61:1–2

Hear my cry, O God;
  listen to my prayer.
From the ends of the earth I call to you,
  I call as my heart grows faint;
    lead me to the rock that is higher than I.

Psalm 62:1–2, & 8

Truly my soul finds rest in God;
  my salvation comes from him.
Truly he is my rock and my salvation;
  he is my fortress, I will never be shaken.

Trust in him at all times, you people;
  pour out your hearts to him,
    for God is our refuge.

Psalm 91:1–2

Whoever dwells in the shelter of the Most High
  will rest in the shadow of the Almighty.
I will say of the Lord, "He is my refuge and my fortress,
  my God, in whom I trust."

Psalm 114: 7 & 8

Tremble, earth, at the presence of the Lord,
  at the presence of the God of Jacob,
who turned the rock into a pool,
  the hard rock into springs of water.

Psalm 125:1–2

Those who trust in the Lord are like Mount Zion,
  which cannot be shaken but endures forever.
As the mountains surround Jerusalem,
  so the Lord surrounds his people both now and forevermore.

Psalm 130:7 (The Message)

O Israel, wait and watch for God—
  with God's arrival comes love,
  with God's arrival comes generous redemption.

Psalm 131:3 (The Message)

Wait, Israel, for God. Wait with hope.
  Hope now; hope always!

Psalm 141:8a

But my eyes are fixed on you, Sovereign Lord;
  in you I take refuge—

Psalm 146:3–6

Do not put your trust in princes,
  in human beings, who cannot save.
When their spirit departs, they return to the ground;
  on that very day their plans come to nothing.
Blessed are those whose help is the God of Jacob,
  whose hope is in the Lord their God.
He is the Maker of heaven and earth,
  the sea, and everything in them—
  he remains faithful forever.

Isaiah 40:11

He tends his flock like a shepherd:
  He gathers the lambs in his arms
and carries them close to his heart;
  he gently leads those that have young.

Isaiah 41:10

So do not fear, for I am with you;
  do not be dismayed, for I am your God.
I will strengthen you and help you;
  I will uphold you with my righteous right hand.

Isaiah 41:13

For I am the Lord your God
  who takes hold of your right hand
and says to you, Do not fear;
  I will help you.

Isaiah 54:10

"Though the mountains be shaken
  and the hills be removed,
yet my unfailing love for you will not be shaken
  nor my covenant of peace be removed,"
  says the Lord, who has compassion on you.

Jeremiah 17:14

Heal me, Lord, and I will be healed;
  save me and I will be saved,
  for you are the one I praise.

Jeremiah 29:11

"For I know the plans I have for you," declares the Lord, "plans to prosper you and not to harm you, plans to give you hope and a future."

Micah 7:7

But as for me, I watch in hope for the Lord,
  I wait for God my Saviour;
  my God will hear me.

Habakkuk 3:17–19

Though the fig tree does not bud
  and there are no grapes on the vines,
though the olive crop fails
  and the fields produce no food,
though there are no sheep in the pen
  and no cattle in the stalls,
yet I will rejoice in the Lord,
  I will be joyful in God my Saviour.
The Sovereign Lord is my strength;
  he makes my feet like the feet of a deer,
  he enables me to tread on the heights.

Zephaniah 3:17

The Lord your God is with you,
  the Mighty Warrior who saves.
He will take great delight in you;
  in his love he will no longer rebuke you,
  but will rejoice over you with singing.

John 15:9–11

As the Father has loved me, so have I loved you. Now remain in my love. If you keep my commands, you will remain in my love, just as I have kept my Father's commands and remain in his love. I have told you this so that my joy may be in you and that your joy may be complete.

John 16:33

I have told you these things, so that in me you may have peace. In this world you will have trouble. But take heart! I have overcome the world.

2 Corinthians 4:18

So we fix our eyes not on what is seen, but on what is unseen, since what is seen is temporary, but what is unseen is eternal.

Philippians 4:13

I can do all this through him who gives me strength.

1 Peter 5:6–7

Humble yourselves, therefore, under God's mighty hand, that he may lift you up in due time. Cast all your anxiety on him because he cares for you.

I John 4:18

There is no fear in love. But perfect love drives out fear, because fear has to do with punishment. The one who fears is not made perfect in love.

Appendix 9

List of the Reflections

Acknowledgements

Many people have contributed to the journey that is described in this book and, therefore, ultimately led to this book; too many to name everyone individually. However, although I cannot name everybody, there are nonetheless quite a few that I would like to thank here.

My contemplative journey began when two friends, Maggie Wallis and Moira McKay, organised the retreat that introduced me to Sandra Holt who subsequently became my Spiritual Director. Sandra has been a faithful and wise companion since 1997. She has spent many hours listening to me and, therefore, with me for God's word in my life. Again and again she has helped me to discern the grace I needed at any one time to fulfil His call to me to be more fully who He has created me to be. She has encouraged and challenged me but always left me free. I am profoundly grateful.

In the wake of our accident, four friends acted on the prompting they felt God gave them to come and pray with James and me in hospital. Their presence created the opportunity for God to speak to my heart and, I believe, enabled me to hear His invitation to trust Him then and now with all that would follow. Thank you to Meg Duncan, Robin Hay, and Andy and Brenda Robertson for their faithful attentiveness to God who led them to our side that evening.

The church stepped out to meet us in our time of need as well. In particular, our local church, Fetteresso Parish Church, has given living expression time and again to what it means for the church to be the bride of Christ in all her radiance through their practical help, their perseverance in prayer, and their abiding concern for us as a family. Thank you for so faithfully standing with us and strengthening us with your love and constancy.

I would like to thank the circle of friends who supported me, week in week out, in response to my Friday text message updates. Through their replies and encouragement, they gave me courage and hope. Through their prayers and the scriptures they sent me, they pointed me continually to the solid foundation of God's love and promises into which I could then lean and know myself held.

Social media and email meant that close and dear friends both near and far away kept abreast of developments and supported us with words of encouragement and, when they could, the gifts of their time and presence. Many enrolled their church families, often our former church families, in prayer for us. We were overwhelmed by the support we received and deeply touched by the kindness that surrounded and enfolded us. Thank you to them all.

Our immediate families gave us enormous support as well. Our parents, our siblings, the boys' cousins all showed their love and concern in countless ways. In particular, my parents, Ann and John Reid, kept the show on the road at home in the early months as they came and lived with us to enable us to come and go more easily. Thank you to them for their love and support at a time which was also difficult for them as this was their grandson and they carried enormous hurt and anguish for him too.

I mentioned in a footnote Sam's friend, Laurie Brown, who visited him nearly every day in hospital in Glasgow. I want to thank Laurie again for his steadfast friendship and support of Sam over those many months. Laurie demonstrated at every visit how to be the best of friends and how to accompany someone in a challenging place by simply showing up and taking it from there. No great demands were placed on Sam during those visits; they would just hang out. Thank you does not begin to capture it – Laurie was and is an exceptional friend.

Many of my friends at church wanted me to write this book and have, therefore, encouraged and supported me with persistent, if gentle, enquiries about how it was going and the progress I was making. They know who they are and I am grateful for their encouragement and belief that this story was worth telling and the benefits of the contemplative journey worth sharing.

Special thanks to those who read it in draft with a specific view to giving me feedback; in particular, Sara Hewins and her Christian book group, Ann Maree Campbell and my sister-in law Polly Dickinson. My thanks go also to Mike Samson for the wonderful cover art and to Ian Shewan for his photographic skill and contributions.

Writing and publishing a book has felt a lot like have a baby and giving birth. My midwives at the end were my sister-in-law, Philippa Dickinson, and graphic designer, Lizzy Laczynska. Their experience, talent and guidance not only reassured me but controlled the pain and ensured the job got done! I am incredibly grateful to them both for their contributions.

Finally, thank you to the boys in my life. Thank you to Andrew for the way he carried on when James and I were caught up in the aftermath of the accident and supporting Sam. He showed extraordinary maturity and gracious love and I am hugely proud of him and the man that he has become.

Thank you to Sam. I know he doesn't like to be considered

extraordinary because, in his eyes, he just gets up and gets on with it. However, in the midst of all that changed for him as a result of this accident, he has not dwelt on the past but shown the way and led from the front, living not for the days to come but for the day that it is given with a hope and gratitude that stand out and don't so much lay down a challenge as an invitation to others to join him in that place. This freedom that he offers those who draw close to him and love him is a rare, precious, and indeed remarkable gift. I am so incredibly proud of who he is.

To James, last but not least, my thanks for reading each draft and for the ensuing guidance and comments but especially for the constant love, patience, and belief in me. He is my closest companion on this adventure that is life and each day is the brighter because of him.

Notes

Notes